GET OUT OF YOUR OWN WAY

GET OUT OF YOUR OWN WAY

10 steps to unlock your true potential

ALEX GOLDIE

Copyright © Alex Goldie 2025

The right of Alex Goldie to be identified as the
Author of the Work has been asserted by him in accordance
with the Copyright, Designs and Patents Act 1988.

First published in 2025 by Headline Welbeck Non-Fiction
An imprint of Headline Publishing Group Limited

1

Apart from any use permitted under UK copyright law, this publication may
only be reproduced, stored, or transmitted, in any form, or by any means, with
prior permission in writing of the publishers or, in the case of reprographic
production, in accordance with the terms of licences issued by
the Copyright Licensing Agency.

Cataloguing in Publication Data is available from the British Library

Hardback ISBN 978 1 0354 2004 9
Trade Paperback ISBN 978 1 0354 2005 6

Typeset in Berling by CC Book Production

Printed and bound in Great Britain by Clays Ltd, Elcograf S.p.A.

Headline's policy is to use papers that are natural, renewable and
recyclable products and made from wood grown in sustainable forests.
The logging and manufacturing processes are expected to conform to
the environmental regulations of the country of origin.

Headline Publishing Group Limited
An Hachette UK Company
Carmelite House
50 Victoria Embankment
London EC4Y 0DZ

The authorised representative in the EEA is Hachette Ireland,
8 Castlecourt Centre, Dublin 15, D15 XTP3, Ireland
(email: info@hbgi.ie)

www.headline.co.uk
www.hachette.co.uk

For Rebecca & Grace, of course

THE 10 STEPS

A Note to All Readers   ix
Introduction   1

1. *Acknowledge and Design Your Own Timeline*   15
2. *Engage With Past Trauma*   45
3. *Get Over Yourself*   69
4. *Grow From Failure*   107
5. *Pull Out the Weeds That Keep Growing Back*   129
6. *Become Accountable*   157
7. *Reject Your Lazy Side*   177
8. *Build Self-Esteem Wherever Possible*   199
9. *Be You as Much as You Can*   231
10. *Do Everything Alone*   253

Acknowledgements   273

A NOTE TO ALL READERS

Some sections of this book explore strategies and insights aimed at fostering confidence and self-assurance, many of which draw upon behaviours and practices, such as those related to body language and eye contact, that relate most closely to the neurotypical experience.

I want to acknowledge that not all readers will find every strategy or perspective applicable to their unique experiences, particularly those who are neurodivergent. If holding eye contact, maintaining specific body language, or any other suggestion in this book feels uncomfortable or unaligned with your personal needs, please know that your confidence and value are not defined by these behaviours.

This book is not meant to prescribe a single path to confidence, but to offer tools that can be adapted to suit many different journeys. Your worth and ability to thrive exist independently of societal norms or expectations, and I encourage you to embrace the approaches that resonate most authentically with you.

Thank you for reading, and I hope you find insights here that empower you in your own way.

INTRODUCTION

For anyone too young to remember, Blockbuster was at one point the world's biggest movie rental company. When a new film came out, after it was released at the cinema but before you could buy your own copy, you could rent it from your local Blockbuster. You could also rent older movies and TV shows. Then along came Netflix. Netflix started out with a similar rental model, though instead of it being a physical store you walked into, they were a postal service where they would mail you the movie and you would then mail it back after you'd watched it. From there, they evolved pretty quickly into an online service, and so began the early days of what has become the Netflix of today. While they were initially low on funding to expand their business model, they were confident about where the movie market was heading, so they contacted Blockbuster. Their proposition was that Blockbuster should purchase Netflix and then Netflix could run the online wing of Blockbuster, which didn't exist at the time.

Blockbuster initially refused the meeting. After all, Blockbuster at that point were making $6 billion in revenue, so why should they care about a small online rental company anyway, right? Netflix were persistent, however, and eventually Blockbuster granted them a last-minute meeting.

Netflix laid out their plan and suggested Blockbuster purchase them for a cool $50 million. Blockbuster laughed them out of the room. But Netflix remained confident about the market and the way it was heading, and about themselves, so they swore to overtake Blockbuster and put them out of business. And eventually they did just that.

As Blockbuster were turning over an impressive six billion dollars, they could easily have created something online that would have rivalled and probably crushed Netflix as it was at the time, but they didn't, because they were lazy, stubborn and arrogant. Blockbuster simply didn't believe that that's where the market was going. They believed the physical store would always be there. They had the chance to do what Netflix did and they blew it. They got in their own way and sunk their own ship. In 2023, Netflix made $33 billion in revenue.

Huge companies may seem like they're massive faceless corporate entities, but ultimately they are run by people. And people do not like to believe they are wrong, which can cause them to back their own position and choices despite any evidence to the contrary. In the case of Blockbuster, it led to

INTRODUCTION

their own destruction, a destruction for which no one was to blame but themselves.

A lot of our own personal issues may not come down to quite the same levels of arrogance or laziness, but there are a multitude of ways in which we too stunt our own growth and act as a barrier to our own happiness and success in life.

Blockbuster had one purpose and that was to entertain the masses with accessible movies, but they failed to live out their purpose long-term. You too have a purpose in this life, and yet you may never see this purpose come to fruition, whether that's because you stumble and give up, or because you don't begin in the first place, instead sitting back and believing that where you are and what you're doing right now is enough to help you fulfil your purpose.

Don't be a Blockbuster. I'm here to help you engage more with the way your life unfurls and, I hope, through this book, to help you get out of your own way.

> 'Understanding is deeper than knowledge. There are many people who know you, but very few who understand you.'
>
> NICOLAS CAGE

Know thyself

How well do you really understand yourself? It's a core belief of mine that a lack of understanding of oneself is at the centre of many of our feelings of stagnation and unhappiness.

Because we are often the masters of our own destruction, a lack of awareness of our culpable nature will cause us to fail in relationships, friendships, career progression and with regards to our overall success. If we don't spend time understanding ourselves, I would argue, it can become all too easy to absorb other people's opinions of us, as we don't have the insight to know who we really are, and thus what it will take to pull us towards what will make us happy. More often than not, the opinions of others will more than likely be incorrect, as they tend to project their own issues onto the situations they see. Knowing who you are at a very deep level is the best way to navigate both the bottom of the pit and the top of the mountain, and will also protect you from too readily accepting the debilitating opinions of others. (More of this in Chapter 5 – Pull Out the Weeds That Keep Growing Back.)

There have been numerous times where a lack of understanding of who I fundamentally am has caused me to achieve nothing, fail and, consequently, made it oh so tempting to stay within my comfort zone. I grew up in an unstable home, an aggressive father, an anxious mother, and surrounded by siblings on all sides, me being the middle child. Being in the middle meant that sometimes I was missed out, either on purpose,

INTRODUCTION

to avoid aggression, or accidentally, because my siblings took the spotlight instead, for both good and bad reasons. I was not given the attention I might have needed, and this led me to think negatively about myself. I slipped into the role of family peacekeeper, as all I wanted was for the aggression to stop, but that wasn't what I wanted to be or what I wanted to do. And it meant I didn't get the time to work out who I was because I was always looking out for everyone else. Unsurprisingly, looking out for everyone else was exhausting and made me lazy in other aspects of my life. I didn't have much interest in school growing up, and socially, I was shy, but I wanted people around me to be happy, so I continued in this role of peacekeeper. Avoid conflict at all costs and make everyone laugh was the aim. I figured that if you never push the boat out, if you don't make too many ripples, then you can happily avoid difficult life conversations and, potentially, any conflict.

This comfort zone became my happy place for most of my life. The problem is, however, that nothing gets done in the comfort zone. You don't become an incredible person, you don't get to experience incredible things, and you don't get to have relationships with incredible people. While my personality and tendencies were born from my experiences, I only realised later (and way too late for my liking) that I could change. I had the power within me to experience a life I wanted and not the one I thought I was destined for because of my past. I hated being shy. I hated not being confident. I hated not knowing what I was capable of. My upbringing was traumatic to a degree, but at some point I realised that *I* was the one keeping myself in that perpetual state. And in trying to understand myself better, and after realising that nobody was coming to save me, I decided to change my life for the better and, ultimately, become free.

When things don't go our way in life, we have a tendency to look outward. We look to blame others, to say it was *their* fault. We assume we're already doing everything we can, because the patterns we've been repeating over and over are all we really know, and so it must be the people around us who are to blame. But they're not. *We* have control over our lives, no one else, and *we* are the reason things haven't worked out so far. A better understanding of oneself on a deeper level can help you navigate life with clearer vision, instead of aimlessly floating along. You will learn to have far better clarity about what you want and how best to go about achieving it. Everything in your life will become better for it: relationships will be easier, friendships will become more enjoyable. And I hope, most importantly, you will finally find a sense of belonging in this world.

There's a saying that 'the truth will set you free', and believe me when I say that only the truest version of you can ever be happy. I know this first-hand from spending years and years trying to be something I'm not, trying to be someone I'm not, just so people would like me. But these same people would reject me over and over, because, really, I had built a fake personality, and after spending a little time with that false edifice, people began to see its lack of authenticity, its lack of honesty and its lack of depth, and clearly that is not the best way to build a connection. This repeated scenario was the case for most of my adult relationships. They would be attracted to this version of

INTRODUCTION

me that I dressed up, and they liked the mask, and the mask either stayed there, preventing any intimacy building, or it slipped and they saw a version of me they didn't like. I was inauthentic so as to get people to like me and then they left me *because* I was inauthentic. This is one of the most unattractive traits to have: to be seen as fake and untrustworthy. Complete honesty is the only way to live, and once you begin to live by this principle, the sense of all that weight lifting off your shoulders will give you a guaranteed high that will carry you through. I'm really excited for you to experience it, but don't get put off about the steps you'll need to take to get there. Change can be a scary experience for anyone used to wearing their fake suit day in, day out, but we will get you to a confident place where you will realise it was never needed in the first place, and then we can build the authenticity naturally from there.

With this book I hope to help you to learn how to strip everything back – every layer you've added to protect yourself from the outside world and your own thoughts. Every layer you've added to try to make people like you more or even so you can like yourself. All the tricks and the lies that have only ever got you so far. It's *all* going to come off. You are going back to your authentic self and that's what you will show to people. You will finally be proud and unapologetically *you*. Because only this version of you can accomplish your goals and only this version of you can truly be happy with yourself when you reach the top of life's hill. And once you're there, there will be no regrets, as you'll have done it all without any lies or manipulation.

I want nothing more than to see you succeed. I want you to be incredibly happy and content with your life. No longer afraid to take those first steps and no longer worrying about how you're going to do it. With my help, I hope you will find a far better understanding of yourself, that you will learn to trust in yourself again, as you once did. I want to instil in you an unwavering belief that you can accomplish what you set out to do, however big or small the task.

Just do me one favour, because this incredible transformation doesn't come easy – nothing worth anything in this world ever comes easily – it may make you feel uncomfortable, and this discomfort may make you feel like this is a struggle, but I promise it is all progress. I want you to try to enjoy the journey while you are on it. Once you get out the other side, you will be proud of yourself, proud of how you handled the highs and lows, so celebrate every step and congratulate yourself on the wins and losses. You'll never quite take a ride like this again – enjoy it.

If you are reading this for the first time, you may find some sections may be more applicable to you than others. I recommend you follow all the steps as they come, and hopefully that should help you reap all the rewards that this book can offer. But I also wanted to write it in such a way that you could also dip in and out, in order to tackle a specific hardship as it happens, say, and so, while I would recommend going through it step-by-step initially, feel free to come back to this book throughout your life as you come across certain challenges.

By picking up this book, though, you have already begun

INTRODUCTION

the process. Something in you must realise you're in need of support in some aspect of your life. So, well done, you're already ahead of the majority of the population. Be proud of your choice.

With this book's help, you'll put a plan in progress for your life and see everything fall into place. How do I know this? Because it's going to be something you've never tried before. We are going to f*ck sh*t up! You will learn and re-learn, try and fail, regress and develop, and in doing all this you will become the happiest human you can be. Many people who get in their own way frequently look at others and think that their good fortune is either just luck or they were born that way, but with the help of this book you'll become one of those people yourself, and then you'll know that's not entirely true, because you'll have seen the work it took to get there.

> 'You're a paradox. You want to be happy, but you think of things that make you sad. You're lazy, yet ambitious. You don't like yourself, but you think others should. You say you don't care but really you do. You crave love but reject it when it comes your way. You're a conflicted contradiction. If you can't figure yourself out, there's no way anyone else can.'
>
> UNKNOWN

Knowing myself

Who the heck are you and how do you know this? You might well ask. Well, I am the son of a violent alcoholic, a cowardly boy who was scared of most experiences. Anxious about the world around me. Always expecting the worst to happen. Too shy to ask, too resigned to believe. I had an addiction to procrastination, an infatuation with my comfort zone. Trying nothing new meant nothing could hurt me. I was protected in my bubble. A needy, clingy, annoying attention-seeker. And all this gave me the space to hate myself. When you hate yourself, you really have reached the bottom. I had just enough strength to keep myself from completely giving up, and it was then that I demanded a change. I studied, I watched, I searched for inspiration in others, and I read. Many incredible books helped me to change it all. I experienced everything life was offering me, and I have come out the other side with only a few cuts and scrapes. My worst fears never materialised, barely anything negative actually happened when I put myself out there. I stopped pretending to live and actually lived. I silenced that anxious mind. I developed some incredible relationships, including with an incredible woman. I shared my hopes and dreams, found motivation and then took action. And after doing all this, I wanted to help people the same way I had once needed help, so I put myself out there with everything I had learned and experienced and created content online for people to enjoy and learn from. I realised I could reach people right at the source of most of their misery and comfort:

INTRODUCTION

social media. And so I disrupted the For You page. People went from swiping through dance and prank videos and suddenly stopped on me, a guy with a big ginger beard offering an alternative way of thinking, giving people their self-belief back, and it went viral. I have currently amassed 2.5 million social media followers and have helped millions more turn their lives around. Social media is fantastic for many reasons – keeping up to date with loved ones and heroes, for a start – but it is definitely a daily kick in the crotch too. You sit there and swipe away, seeing other people live a life that you could only wish for. Doing this repeatedly over a long period of time is damaging to our mental state and so that is why I wanted to create videos to disrupt the narrative. Show people there is a happier side to life. I wanted to bring out a healthier side of social media.

I realised, through my growing platform, that so many others were like the old me. Too scared to take the step, too shy to ask for what they wanted, too nervous of others' opinions. I wanted to change this and realised that I could help people with my knowledge and experience. I could put them on the same incredible path of transformation that I went on.

> 'Lately, I noticed that everybody looks okay until you eventually have a deep conversation with them. And then, you realise that this is a sad generation of people struggling to survive through smiling faces and pretty pictures.'
>
> UNKNOWN

Unfollow your old self

While I love social media, I do believe that it just isn't enough. Even if many people relate to my content, like it, comment on it, engage with it, that doesn't mean that they are fixed and that all will be well now. There is so much information online and even the best of messages can get lost or forgotten. So I thought about how I could enact real change and speak to people in a meaningful way, in a way that won't disappear the second they swipe off. This is what this book was written for. It's an extension of my content but with a deeper understanding, a bigger discussion, and actionable steps and tips to finally bring your life together. The goal for this book is that, after you've lived it and taken this journey with me, you'll be in a place where you can actually *unfollow me*. And while I will miss you, I want you to be in such an incredible place that you no longer need me. This should be the goal for all the self-help industry. I'm not peddling a drug that you need to keep coming back to me for. I'm giving you a solution. I want to you to experience the life you've always pined for and, let's be honest, I doubt my big ginger beard on your screen was ever actually in that dream.

I initially thought writing this book would be difficult, but it became pretty easy when I asked myself: what did I need to hear when I didn't know what to do with my life? What guidance did I need when I was incredibly anxious, being crushed under the weight of insecurities and filled with self-doubt? There was so much that I didn't know about my mental health,

INTRODUCTION

so much I didn't understand about myself throughout my teens and twenties. That's the beauty of the human experience: there are always chances to learn.

And, while I loved my journey in finding myself and achieving success, it would have been very useful and meant a lot less pain and hurt if I could have found all the answers I was looking for in one place. So that's exactly what this book is. It's for you – it's your one-stop shop for everything you need to know about how to get out of your own way, achieve your dreams and become happy and content in this life. Everything in this book is what got me to my own happy and successful place in this life, and so I hope you can absorb it all and so experience your own incredible journey. I'm delighted to be on it with you.

Now, let's get started.

1
ACKNOWLEDGE AND DESIGN YOUR OWN TIMELINE

> 'We are all in different time zones. Just because one person's ahead doesn't mean you're behind. Some find their path early, others later. Some start careers at 22, some at 62. Success and fulfilment don't follow a set schedule. You're not late, you're just in your own time zone.'
>
> ALEX GOLDIE

You are neither late nor too early to achieve anything

You're not late, nor are you too early, you're exactly where you're supposed to be. Right here with me. We start out living a fixed timeline, through childhood and school. Go to nursery/kindergarten, then on to primary school and so on. This timeline is created for us, manufactured by a mixture of government rules and societal expectations, and then demonstrated to us by our parents. All of this is done to give you the best chance to live a normal life thereafter. The timeline is structured, purposeful and completely out of your control. Then we hit our late-teens (for some, it's 16, for others, 18), and we are given the opportunity to control our own timeline.

With our whole life ahead of us and having been controlled for most of our lives so far, what do the majority of people do in this situation? Not a lot actually. Most will then experience the next ten years without much thought at all. They will experience life and live each moment as they come, without much of a plan. Of course, this is not necessarily a problem, and maybe some people aren't ready to decide yet. However, there is a reason people often reach their late-twenties and panic. They see what everyone else around them is achieving: great careers, starting families or even travelling. The famous quarter-life crisis kicks in (more on this later) and they question everything, leaving them lost and disengaged with life and society.

This is because there's an undercurrent of competition within our societies, a fear of being left behind, and a jealousy of others if they are seen as further ahead. We see other people's lives within our age groups and assume that we should be at the same stage as them, on the same trajectory as them. But I call bullsh*t.

This panic and uncertainty will only cause you to make rash decisions. Either forcing you into something you're not ready for

ACKNOWLEDGE AND DESIGN YOUR OWN TIMELINE

yet or even something that's not right for you. Or you don't do anything at all, and thus stay stagnant and unhappy in life. You can easily end up just floating in indecision and waste even more time. What is important to understand here is that everyone is on a timeline, but everyone is on a *different* timeline.

Everyone's timeline will be different, everyone will take various lengths of time to achieve things, and this is because of varying factors. The varying factors could be how much free time you have, how much you apply yourself, if you have a family to support, the materials you have available to you and what kind of support you have around you. Don't get it twisted, though – these aren't excuses as to why you can't achieve something, they may simply affect how long it takes to achieve your goals, and this is why we all need to plan out a timeline ahead of us. I want you to remember there is absolutely nothing wrong with taking a while to do something, but not making *any* steps to progress will naturally cause stagnation. What most commonly happens is that we let the fear of missing out take control and so get in the way of ourselves when we should actually be planning our own timeline, setting goals, taking steps and trusting the process.

So, in this chapter, we are going to set ourselves a timeline and promise ourselves we are going to stick to it. To break it down, you will have need at least two timelines: one will be your Overall Timeline and the other (or others) will be your timeline(s) of success in individual fields. Let's start with your Overall Timeline because it requires less planning and will hopefully become a constant mental state in your life.

Your Overall Timeline

Your Overall Timeline is designed to shift your way of thinking from 'I hope this happens' to 'I know it will', and help you trust that you are on the right path. This timeline is unique to you, and certain big life events – like finding the career of your dreams or starting a family – can happen at no particular set time. But if you want these things to happen at all, then they have to be on your timeline, because, really, how else are they going to come your way?

And once they're on your timeline, you have to trust that they will happen. Quite simply, having this trust in your own timeline is there to ensure you avoid experiencing daily anxiety and/or prevent you attempting any rogue moves out of the anxiety that your goals are either not going to happen or that you're not doing enough to achieve them.

Of course, nothing comes from nothing, and we aren't just going to sit on our butts, blissfully ignorant and thinking all will come to us without us having to lift a finger. No, we will be working towards achieving our goals, but it's good for us all to know that it's okay if some days we take tiny steps and some days we take giant leaps. It doesn't matter if most days are tiny steps (more on this later), but we are not to worry and get bent out of shape if things aren't happening overnight or straightaway.

The other reason it's important to be confident in your timeline is that it will keep you motivated to take the tiny steps. I

ACKNOWLEDGE AND DESIGN YOUR OWN TIMELINE

imagine it as being like a slow hike to the top of a mountain. You will eventually get to the point you want, where you don't need to worry about whether it will actually happen, where you trust that it will, because you're doing something to make it happen. Again, anxiety has no place within your timeline, so banish that for ever.

Having an Overall Timeline also protects you from experiencing bouts of jealousy. Currently, in our age of social media, we can see and watch everything that anyone has ever achieved, whether that's public figures or your friends. Seeing those friends achieve milestones that you also covet will then make you jealous, which will in turn become damaging for your own mental health. This is where your timeline comes in, because it will ensure you believe in your heart that you will also experience these things, even if it is in your own time. But, equally, remember that the reason these people have achieved something at this exact time is because it was part of their own, very separate timeline. There is a very high chance that you have accomplished or done something on your timeline already that they would like to achieve just as much, but the only way you avoid becoming bitter or letting envy get the better of you is to congratulate those friends, smile and know that you yourself are working towards a similar experience.

> ### Making an Overall Timeline
>
> This is going to be a lot simpler than you thought. Sit down with a pen and paper, or open the Notes section of your phone, if you feel like that will either make it easier to do (whichever will help you remember what you've written and whatever will motivate you more). Then write down what you would like to achieve in your life. It's really that simple. It can be as long or short, as grand or modest as you'd like. Welcome to your Overall Timeline!

Your smaller timelines

How often do you hear 'oh, what's the point in starting [insert goal]? I'll be 30 before I'm finished.' Something people often neglect to remember is you'll be 30 before you know it anyway. So why not be 30/40/50/60 with the goal achieved?

Your other timelines are smaller ones. These aren't goals you hope to achieve across your whole life, but ones that you have shorter-term deadlines for. They can be singular or working in parallel with each other. They can just be trying to work on one thing (let's say write a book . . . no idea why that's on my mind!). And it's fine to focus on a single thing, but you may also have other, smaller timelines running simultaneously, like getting in healthier shape, becoming a fantastic parent or overcoming your social anxiety. While you work daily or weekly to

ACKNOWLEDGE AND DESIGN YOUR OWN TIMELINE

achieve these short-term goals, they will be more than likely helping you to work towards your Overall Timeline goals too. For example, your short-term goal of overcoming social anxiety, whilst it's on a smaller timeline, is actually helping towards your Overall Timeline goal of meeting the person of your dreams.

I recently purchased my first home (whoo, go me!). To be honest with you, while I have always wanted to own instead of rent (Overall Timeline), I spent most of my life never taking the goal seriously. I didn't think, in this day and age, and with the amount I earned, I would ever be able to afford it (as I had allowed my defeatist mindset to get in the way). I could have been saving, but because I never believed in the goal, I wasted the money on other things. Something triggered me, though . . . rent in London has become extortionate. I decided that I could and I would buy a home, and that it didn't matter if it took me another ten years to get in a position to do it. I placed being more intelligent with my money on my Smaller Timeline, set out a plan and watched it build, until I eventually achieved my Overall Timeline goal too. It took me five years. But it wouldn't have mattered if it took me ten years. The beauty and difficulty of time is how rapidly it passes. Five years seemed for ever away, but looking back now, it only really feels like a year ago. So while it's good to give yourself rough deadlines to achieve these goals by, I would encourage you not to worry about how long something takes exactly, as when it comes to fruition, you'll just be thankful that you started and made the necessary steps.

By definition of being on shorter timelines, these goals will take a bit more concentration and daily work. Let's use social anxiety again as an example. Say you currently struggle with social outings or being forced to meet new people in work or at school. Being tired of this, you want to turn it around. You want to become confident in social situations, you want to be someone that people are actually interested in and want to get to know you better. You want to be wittier and more charismatic. So, you set out a plan and this plan will have a timeline. This timeline may have no exact timescale; you can tell yourself you want to achieve this in one year, but, equally, you'll be okay if you achieve it quicker or if it takes longer. Again, setting a target date is important to track progress, but don't beat yourself up if you haven't achieved the goal in the time, provided you have been working at it. If you haven't been doing anything towards this goal, however, feel free to pinch yourself . . . one of those real painful little nips your brother used to give. I have five siblings, so I got nipped. Just focus on the steps – small or big, it doesn't matter. You'll research ways to overcome social anxiety and put the plan into action. For social anxiety, it may look like reading and watching content that offers tips and advice for people with social anxiety and then practicing them in public. No doubt it'll mean pushing yourself out of your comfort zone and exposing yourself to your fear, since a lot of goal-achievement does involve this (more on this later).

Using what you learn from doing this, either continue the good work or adjust things that didn't work out, but never, ever give up. It's also wise to have check-ins with yourself on

ACKNOWLEDGE AND DESIGN YOUR OWN TIMELINE

a weekly and/or monthly basis to see how you're improving. Sometimes, when we are going through the motions, we end up neglecting the progress we're making, but with a check-in, you can see that you are improving, which gives you a boost to carry on. And just like with our Overall Timeline, we won't get disheartened if it doesn't happen overnight. You have to trust it will happen and that you will achieve this dream because it's on your timeline. You're making the steps and it's now only a matter of when, not if.

Planning smaller timelines

Using your Overall Timeline as inspiration to show you what you ultimately want to achieve, think about what you would need to do and the smaller steps you need to achieve in order to reach each of those larger goals. Write down a series of smaller timelines and, next to them, roughly when you would hope to achieve them by. This is what you follow each day and how you plan out what you're going to put your time and energy into.

'You're crazy until you're successful.'

JIMMY DONALDSON, AKA MR BEAST

You have no limit

Humans are impressive; we've achieved and created quite unimaginable things. We've built the pyramids, invented wireless internet and, at some point, Raffaele Esposito baked some dough with cheese and tomato and created the first pizza. So many incredible things thought up by so many apparently incredible people. But here is many people's first mistake. Why are these things only created by incredible people? And the short answer is they aren't. Anybody who has achieved or created anything impressive in this world only becomes incredible after the fact. Only *after* they invent the nail or create the recipe for Coca-Cola do they achieve incredible status.

We live in a society where we put people on pedestals after we see the usefulness of their invention, and it's at that moment that we see them as brilliant humans and assume they must have been so all along. We naturally think these people must have been the smartest students in school, and that they must have been born super geniuses and, yes, in some cases they are, but in the majority of cases . . . definitely not!

I'm currently reading Stephen King's book *On Writing* (yes, the irony is not lost on me). In this semi-autobiography, King goes into detail about his failures. When we think about someone as successful as Stephen King, it's hard to imagine that he wasn't always successful. King is now seen as a genius in the horror fiction world, having had numerous bestsellers and many of his novels converted into big box-office movies.

ACKNOWLEDGE AND DESIGN YOUR OWN TIMELINE

But this is all after the fact. He spent years writing without making a dime. One of his most beloved pieces of work, which is now widely regarded as brilliant, was *Carrie*. But originally he wrote three pages and threw it in the trash. His wife, thankfully, later found it and encouraged him to finish it, but then it was rejected by over 30 different publishers. King was low on confidence and struggling to provide for his family. Nobody knew who the heck Stephen King was – something most of us can relate to. But he didn't give up because he loved writing, and he kept doing it. Becoming a writer was on his timeline and he made the consistent but small steps to achieving it. It took him 20 years to be a success. Eventually, a publisher discovered *Carrie* and saw its potential. I can't speak for Stephen King, but I doubt he cares now how long it took.

This is a secret that nobody talks about: these 'incredible' people that have created these incredible things are actually just regular humans like you or me. Anybody can come up with an idea or a plan. What maybe sets them apart is that when they had an idea or had some sort of inspiration, they didn't drop it. They chased it to fruition, regardless of how long it took and regardless of what people thought.

I know you may not believe it at this very moment, but you are very much capable of creating and achieving amazing things. You just need to know what you want, you need a plan, and you need a timeline, and having a timeline will push you to stay with your dreams and goals regardless of if people (even if that is you) think you're crazy.

> 'Your worst enemy isn't a person, situation, or thing. It's the story in your mind based on assumptions and projected fears or insecurities.'
>
> VEX KING

Eliminate doubt

I've already discussed how having and trusting your timeline will help you with jealousy, but there are even more important reasons for having your timeline. The most important benefit is that it eliminates doubt. Doubt in yourself or your future.

One of our biggest obstacles is not trusting ourselves. Genuinely doubting ourselves seems to be something that most people suffer from, so you are at least not alone in this. This might be because of our previous experiences, where we've attempted to achieve something before and it didn't go as expected, or maybe we were told we weren't good enough as a child and never praised. Either of these experiences, or a multitude of other factors in our past, will cause us to have self-doubt. And the devastating outcome is that we just don't try again – we start to believe we aren't good enough, or we are convinced that this won't be any different than the last time, so why even bother putting ourselves out there?

Even today I still need to remind myself of my timeline and to believe in it. If a piece of content I've worked hard on and thought will help lots of people then doesn't do very well or

ACKNOWLEDGE AND DESIGN YOUR OWN TIMELINE

the message is missed, I get disheartened. I take a moment and too often decide to tell myself I'm not good at this (of course this is me getting in my own way again). Luckily, I've been on this horse before, so I give myself a mental slap and I tell myself to trust in my timeline, as I've witnessed it change my life multiple times. My Overall Timeline goal of becoming a successful content creator is not damaged because some of my videos are not successful. I have to then turn to my Smaller Timeline and keep researching and creating content I believe will help people. I may have a moment of doubt (I am human, and it will happen), but I put this down to receiving minimal praise as a child. Thankfully, it never lasts very long and, luckily, I generally get to prove the doubt wrong pretty quickly with my actions.

This is where I believe your timeline comes into its own. Because your story and timeline are never finished and that means you can keep going. Anyone's timeline, yours included, will involve down moments, moments when you struggle, moments when things don't go the way you thought they would. But trusting in the plan you have put in place, regardless of the low moments, means that you will soon laugh in places where you have previously cried, have trust that you have put your life in motion, and know that you are making the steps towards the reward and that good things are coming.

That's why going off your timeline is dangerous. If you start making decisions based on how you feel in this exact moment, rather than taking into account your whole life, you start making rash decisions, without really thinking about the consequences. Yes, changing jobs or relationships is sometimes a good thing, and deciding to pack it all in and travel the world for a year can be liberating, but when making these decisions on the spur of the moment there is usually a reverberating outcome down the line, one that has an unplanned effect on your timeline and that can stunt your growth.

Take the 90/10 rule of dating as an example. This rule states that when you're in a relationship with someone that gives you 90% of everything you want but there's this 10% that's not there, and one day you meet someone else that has that thing that was the 10%, you can think they're perfect for you because it can feel that this is all you've been missing from your life. You can become so laser-focused on this 10% you neglect to realise that this new person doesn't have the other 90%. You make an instant decision that you obviously live to regret, because now you don't have so much of what you originally wanted.

If we look at jobs, we see the same thing. Let's imagine the job you currently hold isn't fulfilling you and isn't in line with your goals and dreams. There is a temptation to quit, but the more sensible option is to plan. Instead of panicking and leaving to go all in on what you want, you decide what it is you want to achieve, and you research how best to do that. The majority of the time that involves working on a side hustle alongside your existing job until it starts growing. If there is no other line of work that will help you achieve your dream, then you could decide to become comfortable doing this or any other job, as long as it allows you the time to create and progress on your goals on the side of the new venture. Now

ACKNOWLEDGE AND DESIGN YOUR OWN TIMELINE

your timeline involves you achieving this dream, and as a result you are happy with your life, because you know you are moving towards your goals.

Dr Siraj Dokadia, the sales expert, when discussing the link between planning and successful career progression, states: 'One of the primary benefits of planning is that it helps to clarify goals and objectives. Without a plan, it can be difficult to determine what steps are necessary to achieve your desired outcome.'

This idea of having a plan of action instead of winging it is important because it will help you avoid making impulsive decisions that could ultimately hinder your progress. You can just focus on the plan and see it to fruition before changing plan or pivoting.

Remember, there is no need to panic: you have everything covered. You don't have to wake up feeling useless, thinking you have no control, because everything is moving forward on the timeline that you set out. So get rid of that doubt.

What is it you want to achieve?

A big stumbling block for a lot of people is they don't actually know what it is they want. If you're in the minority that have always known, then that's incredible. So much of what stops us is the anxiety of choice. We constantly ask ourselves 'Is this right for me? What if it's a mistake?' Knowing what you want removes a huge headache, and if you're one of those lucky people who are sure, you may not have realised it, but you're already on your timeline and only some better understanding and careful planning of your timeline is required.

However, if you're in the majority (and this was me for most of my life), you probably don't have a clue about what you really want.

Maybe you followed a path you thought was right. A degree in a certain field, because that's what the 15-year-old you wanted for your life, but now your life is different and you don't subscribe to that line of thinking anymore. You may equally have decided that more education was a nightmare scenario and wanted to start making money, but then a few years later you regret not persevering with university for the chance to earn more money in a different line of work.

Another problem you might be experiencing, and this is in all cultures, is you have followed a life path that you feel nothing for because it was what your parents wanted for you. You may have done so because you believed it was in your own best interests, or you may have done so believing it would impress them and please them (or a subtle combination of both).

But one thing we need to keep reminding ourselves of as we try to plot out our own timeline is that this is *our* life and no one else's, and if we make life choices based on other people's expectations and perceptions of us, we become unaligned with and uninterested in our own life. We may realise this quickly, but sometimes it can be years and years later that we discover we weren't really listening to ourselves. (I will discuss in greater

ACKNOWLEDGE AND DESIGN YOUR OWN TIMELINE

detail the involvement of others in our lives in Chapter 5 – Pull Out the Weeds That Keep Growing Back).

Regardless of what path you attempted to take, if you are still stumped as to what to do with your life, the quick and easy option is to try out a few things and see what sticks. This might work well, but I don't think you're reading this chapter because you want to do or attempt just anything, and this book isn't about quick and easy, so the only real option now is to imagine and then reach for something lofty: the career, the ambition or goal that you dream about. The one that you daydream about becoming or experiencing, the one that makes you feel happy imagining it and then instantly depressed because it's not your reality. That's the one. That is what we are going to achieve. Regardless of its absurdity or your conviction that it's just a delusion.

Kill your darlings

One great way to work out what you really want is to write down what others expect of you and then, with that in front of you, see if it's actually something you want. So sit down, think about your parents, your school friends, your colleagues and even that guy in the supermarket queue that seemed to be very disappointed in you for some reason, and write down what you think each one of them expects of you. Now, ask yourself, really ask yourself ... is that what you want to do?

> 'I used to be so delusional. I always imagined I could be more than I was, and eventually I grew and evolved into that person.'
>
> LADY GAGA

Why do you want to achieve this?

I love people with big aspirations, and seeing those people succeed in something that others thought was delusional is wonderful. However, there is a very important caveat that I want to add. It's not meant to diminish any dreams or make you question whether this is the right timeline to embark on, no. All it is is one fairly big question: why do you want this?

In order to truly understand your timeline, you need to ask yourself why you want to achieve this dream and whether you are doing it for the right reasons. I'm sure, for the majority of you, there is good reasoning behind what you want, but you do need to be careful about doing certain things for the wrong reasons. Are you actually doing this to impress others? Are you doing this to make your parents happy? Or are you doing this to have control over others or to spite someone else? None of these reasons will fulfil you – you won't walk away feeling complete.

An example of this I see often is when someone ends a relationship in a bitter way and one or both of them want to achieve something afterwards to make the other jealous

ACKNOWLEDGE AND DESIGN YOUR OWN TIMELINE

or regret the breakup. I went through a breakup; I came out feeling uneasy and unconfident in myself. She had never commented on my physical appearance, but I decided I was going to throw myself into going to the gym to build that revenge body. And I did, but it didn't last very long, because I didn't get the validation I was craving in the end. I was never going to. The 'revenge body' is a house built on sand, i.e. one without a solid foundation, so there was no ongoing motivation to keep me going back. However, if I had decided to go to the gym to become more confident in who I was, become healthier and then happier with myself because of my life choices, then the body and the gym routine would feel rewarding and therefore stand a much better chance of lasting.

It's funny how much we can focus on what others think, but when all is said and done, it never fulfils us. We never get the response we want, and we never feel good about the accomplishment because it wasn't done for us, for our true self. You need to be planning and enjoying your timeline because you yourself want this change, because you are tired of your current pattern and want to create something new, something good that will benefit the most important person in your timeline: you.

Pain points (motivation)

Throughout our lives we all notice things we want to change. It can be just a casual thought, when you spot something you don't have but want, for example, or it can come from some form of scheduled introspection, as with a New Year's resolution. Every year, everyone cries 'New Year, New Me', but so many of these resolutions either last no longer than January or never take flight at all. The more people I speak to through my platform, the more I believe that this is because there is no real pain behind the want and so the need for change goes unanswered.

Pain points are one of the only true ways to evoke real change. People may want to become more confident or get better at dating, but they don't want to become more confident for the sake of it and they don't want to get better at dating just to go on more dates. The real reason for wanting something tends to have a deeper meaning and this is the pain point. People can want to be more confident because they are tired of being walked all over or not being seen. They can want to get better at dating because they are tired of being so bloody lonely. When you try to change because of your pain point, you are far less likely to give up because you are genuinely sick of the circumstances causing the pain. Noticing these pain points, or recalling the memories that inspired them, means you can use them to keep you fighting for change or prevent you from slipping into old habits.

So, what is your pain point? What is this burning motivation? For me, the chaotic home that I was born into led to me identifying as a 'nice guy', out of a desire to please others. Throughout my teens and twenties, this 'Nice Guy syndrome' led to me convincing myself that most men are aggressive meat

ACKNOWLEDGE AND DESIGN YOUR OWN TIMELINE

heads and, if I was a nice guy to all, then everyone would like me, especially the women I was attracted to. Now, don't get me wrong, being a nice person is a good thing, but you should be nice for the right reasons and confident with it. I was nice to make people like me, which is manipulative. I wasn't being nice because that's who I wanted to be, I was being nice to avoid conflict and to impress, and as you can probably guess, that doesn't go so well for you in the real world. People take advantage of anyone too malleable (as being nice makes you), you never get what you actually want (because your wants are a reflection of others' desires), and so my girlfriends either grew tired of someone so placid or they saw through the act and suddenly they saw me as dishonest.

Many people find themselves playing this same role, and they become either too scared to break out of the shell or oblivious to the personality shift in the first place, and then sit wondering why they don't get what they want, frustrated with the people around them, while other seemingly undeserving people do, and then they blame anyone else but themselves. This was my pain point, the point at which I felt the most pain, and so this is where my growth started for me. I wanted out, I wanted to change, I wanted to be authentic; and, after I had achieved this, I wanted to help others do the same.

A common pain point is generational poverty: seeing your parents and grandparents work their arses off only to get a minor return, stuck in a cycle of financial instability. And you want that to change, you want to help them, and you certainly don't want that for yourself and your children. If you've felt this pain for long enough, you will change it. You will place getting out of this difficult financial situation on your timeline and you will see it change. This pain point will light a fire under you and motivate you to achieve this dream. The same goes for anyone looking to be happier who has grown up in an unhappy home. And anyone looking for more confidence and self-esteem. Facing daily reminders of low confidence and experiencing regular scenarios that don't go the way you want them to because you have no love for yourself will become a pain point in your life that makes you want different. Pain points are not exclusive to these examples, but I want to show you what really motivates people for change.

And hard as it is to hear, your true motivator in achieving anything great will more than likely be born from a pain point. You may have one or a few, but, either way, these are your motivation for change and will often be the reason for real success in what you're looking to achieve. Knowing your pain point, while an uncomfortable line of enquiry for anyone, will allow you to complete the goal within your timeline, and exposure to it will motivate you to complete your dream. It is time to use your pain for greatness.

Lucas Mattiello, confidence coach, wrote in his blog, 'Level Up Living': 'Pain was my motivator to change as I reached a point where the feeling of being limited became overwhelming and was greater than the discomfort of changing. This is when I knew that I was ready to make a successful life change.'

If you want to create lasting change identify the *why*. Identify your pain point. This will make your process clearer.

ACKNOWLEDGE AND DESIGN YOUR OWN TIMELINE

Now you have to ask yourself what is it that you know that you can't continue experiencing, what *must* change, what is it that, if it was either no more or became your reality, would change your life drastically and for the better.

Finding the pain

I want you to write down an accurate a statement about what it is you want to change. Then, write down what motivates you to make that change. Put this reminder somewhere you can see it often, whether it's a Post-it note next to your bed or on your fridge. If it's on your phone, then change your phone background to it. A regular reminder of this is all the motivation you'll need to action the change.

Once you've worked it out, this is now an inherent part of your timeline, and it's going to help you make the changes you need. All in good time, though.

This is not a race

We want it but we want it *now*. So much of what we want is given to us instantly in easy dopamine hits. Want to feel good? Have a drink. Want to distract yourself from feeling sad? Scroll on social media. So, when it comes to wanting a change in our lives, and because we expect our experiences of feeling good to come instantly, we are impatient and get discouraged when we don't see the change quickly.

Eckhart Tolle when discussing the concepts in his book, *The Power of Now*, said: 'The mental projection towards the future creates the stresses between, "I'm here, but I want to be there." And for many humans, that is their predominant state. And so, you need to realise most humans have this inbuilt dysfunction. They cannot acknowledge the present moment.'

I agree with Eckhart because I know for myself that I often and incorrectly put importance on what I want in my future over what I am currently experiencing. Often I put a lot of mental capacity into worrying and wishing it was all happening now instead of trusting I will experience it at some point and just enjoy the work and journey towards it.

As we discuss your goals, I want to stress that they will not all come instantly. I get it – it's difficult because you're excited. Anytime anyone starts something new, they want to see the results instantly. It's not your fault we live in a society of instant gratification, where, if you feel down, you can get an instant dopamine hit via your phone, food or alcohol. A quick hit and everything will feel okay again, for a little while. Given all this, it is natural that when we embark on something that really will benefit us but don't see results instantly, we become dissatisfied and bored. A destructive cycle we've all had to cope with most of our lives. If we haven't already talked ourselves out of something before attempting it, and then we actually had a go but then see no change, then it is likely we

ACKNOWLEDGE AND DESIGN YOUR OWN TIMELINE

will quit. I have laid out some steps at the end of this chapter to help you avoid this.

Your timeline is in place to remind you that this dream or goal of yours will happen, even if it does take time, and hopefully, it will even teach you that time is the only way that you will accomplish this goal. Forget every failed attempt and keep going.

Let's use working out as an example, because most people can literally see the change over time. When you start working out consistently, within a month many will see a change in their physique, but their body isn't suddenly going to become a replica of a Greek god. No, to do that, it will require time, consistency and dedication. People may try to rush the process, i.e. they'll have never gone to the gym and then suddenly start working out two times a day, six days a week, but if they do that they are likely to either burn out, because it's exhausting, going from nothing to so much, or they injure themselves (because their body isn't prepared for the sudden shift in activity) and then have to stop. What these people don't realise is they could have achieved their goal by actually doing *less* work, by setting out a commitment to working out or doing some form of exercise three to four times a week, and over time they would have reached their goal of the ideal body without any issues.

It's best not to expect any goal or ambition to be completed quickly. We aren't looking for cheat codes, as this journey will shape you and these skills take time to harness. An expert in anything is just someone who has attempted, failed and completed something multiple times, not just someone who is born with a natural gift.

In the world of professional sports, there is a proverbial graveyard in the hundreds of thousands of people naturally talented at something, but they never make it to the big time – they achieve at an early age with this talent but then do not nurture it, do not adapt and do not practise it.

Similarly, in the real world, people who live too much for the initial burst of progress and don't stick with the training they need to do are likely to fail. Someone who decides to become less socially anxious, for example, will get a little boost the first few times from being more socially confident, but that doesn't mean they've made a permanent change.

We need to aspire to become masters and that means living and breathing our ambitions, rather than just following the ebb and flow of how we feel in the moment. We need to practise our craft so much that it *becomes* us. It's not an overnight thing, but nothing worthwhile ever is.

> 'Maybe not now, but one day your choices will take you where you need to be.'
>
> S. S. SHIVANI

ACKNOWLEDGE AND DESIGN YOUR OWN TIMELINE

The compound effect

The compound effect is a unique way of thinking long-term. It looks at how the small changes and decisions we make today impact us in a big way in the future. The blog Habitify sums it up nicely:

Compound Effect = Choices + Behaviour + Habits + Time

And to accompany it, they say 'The strategy for reaping huge rewards from small changes requires patience, responsibility, and accountability. To make the compound effect work, we need to make the right choices, show the right behaviour, cultivate the best habits, and allow time to take its course.'

This is what I mean when I say it doesn't matter if you only take a small step. Provided you make these steps regularly, the outcome can be massive. Sometimes we can look at our goals and ambitions and get daunted by the size of them, but if we break them down into smaller manageable actions, spread out over a period of time, they become achievable. The way I want you to use your timeline is with this compounding effect. Take your goal and promise to work on it every day, but don't worry if some or all days are small steps. You will get to the prize eventually. The only way you fail is by giving up completely.

Let's use your career as an example. Change is incremental and, in aiming for the dream career, you likely won't realise that you're actually getting closer to the job, even if you can't measure it in the mirror or with numbers. You'll just be doing something each day that gets you into a position from which you can get an interview or a promotion, working every day on building yourself into that perfect candidate. Your only reassurance that you're doing the right thing may be actually getting the job at the end, and this is a hard realisation as throughout you'll need to have trust in yourself that doing these small acts of building every day is getting you closer to your goal.

But, trust me, as long as you promise yourself to do something, even the smallest of somethings, every day until you see it through, regardless of if it takes a while, the compound effect will do the rest. It's never good to rush.

What do you need to do to achieve this?

Once you have chosen your goal and placed it on your timeline, now you need to decide how you will interact with it. Initially setting out your plan for the short term and moving onto what you can do long term as you progress.

Start with your pain point from before, the statement you wrote out. What can you do in the short term (Small Timeline) to negate this pain and what is the overarching goal (Overall Timeline).

What are the steps, small or otherwise, each day that you need to take? Will they be studying, reading, practising, difficult conversations, or exposure therapy?

ACKNOWLEDGE AND DESIGN YOUR OWN TIMELINE

Depending on your goal, a different practice will have to be put in place. Something achievable and something you think you'll be able to do every single day (with the occasional breaks if you need them). Write these down next to the activity in question.

Then you should plan to have check-ins at weekly, monthly or yearly points. Take stock of your progress at these points. Use these check-ins as motivation to keep going and use these moments to celebrate your journey and success along the way.

You must give yourself at least 20 days before you see any small amounts of change. Then at least 90 days to see solid change. For full-scale change, you could be looking at a year to any number of decades to see the complete change. And the bigger the change, the longer this will take. Real change takes time, so be patient.

And at significant check-ins, I also recommend taking at least one bigger step towards your goal. Once a month or year, do something that really gets you out of that comfort zone and gets you noticeably closer. While this might sound scary now, it won't seem so when you've been making your small steps consistently towards this dream. The small steps will give you the confidence to push yourself.

Finally, so you don't forget, set reminders all over the place, in your home and on your phone. They will keep you consistent.

A matter of time

After a consistent period of following and living your timeline, I don't doubt you will be living your dream. But, for now, you are on the right path, and you should be bloody proud of yourself. With the compounding effect of your small actions, it is only a matter of time and time alone that stands in the way of you achieving something incredible.

2

ENGAGE WITH PAST TRAUMA

NOTE: What I discuss here can be triggering, and any advice given is not meant to replace help from a licensed professional.

> 'No amount of guilt can solve the past. No amount of anxiety can change the future.'
>
> UMAR IBN AL-KHATTAB

Everything you've ever experienced

I was born into aggression, the house I grew up in was always on edge. What mood would my dad be in today? Anyone who has grown up with an aggressive parent can attest to how this has influenced them, and this trauma has certainly had an effect on me. It is a trauma that loves to make an appearance in my life in a variety of ways (this I will discuss in more detail later), and particular moments and memories from my childhood which I won't put into print have a funny way of making their way into my everyday thoughts.

When people discuss trauma, the mind tends to go instantly to the worst of life events, which is why I naturally gravitated towards one especially bad instance from my past. However, trauma can be a complex variety of life events and can even come from how certain events add together. And what needs to be understood more widely is that all levels of trauma, great or small, can be debilitating.

That means everything from rejection from a love interest to being dumped by a long-term partner, from work disappointments to being fired from a job. This is all trauma, and this can all have a significant effect on both our present and our future. Simply put, trauma is an emotional response to an overwhelming physical or emotional event. And nobody else can belittle the life experiences that you find traumatic, as we all react differently to different situations.

Some traumas you may never realise you've experienced. These could have been moments from childhood that you don't remember or have simply blocked out. However, they will more than likely show up in your current life; you just may not recognise the ripples of the past until you get to the present day.

Leading treatment centre, The Guest House in Ocala, wrote in an article on their website that helps adults struggling with everyday life because of trauma in childhood, explains it in this way: 'The relationship between trauma and social anxiety

ENGAGE WITH PAST TRAUMA

disorder can impede your well-being in adulthood. Moreover, types of childhood trauma like emotional abuse and neglect can contribute to social anxiety that impairs your ability to function in your daily life and build healthy close relationships.'

The real key here is that past trauma has a huge reverberating effect on our lives, usually compounding self-doubt, low confidence and acceptance of poor circumstances. Your life never really goes anywhere because your traumatic experiences are holding you back. But I want to help you with that.

What I want you to gain from this chapter is how to anchor your past trauma and use it to propel you forward. If I had not experienced what I had during my childhood, I might never have come to this path I'm now on, never wanted to help people with confidence, never started my social media platforms and never begun to help others better their lives. So, all is not lost just because you've experienced trauma. There is a way to take your traumatic experiences, flip them on their head, and create something inspirational and powerful from them. And I'm going to show you exactly how to do that.

Trauma has wrapped itself around your leg and won't let go

I previously alluded to the fact that my past traumas love to make an appearance from time to time, but what I mean by this is not that my past comes back to haunt me, or that I get flashbacks of traumatic life events I've experienced. You won't see me suddenly go silent because I'm thinking about how I got dumped by an ex-girlfriend in front of my best friends (yep, that happened). No, what happens, and usually after the fact, is that it shows up in how I interact with people and the choices I make.

As I write this, my girlfriend is being quiet. She's taking some time to herself, processing something she's anxious about that has absolutely nothing to do with me. But my past experiences of being dumped (more times than I'm willing to admit) are screaming at me, telling me to act in a certain way around her, or else the result could be that she dumps me. This is because, of course, my history has incorrectly told me that her silence is about *me*, and I must do something to make sure she still loves me and doesn't want to leave me. The most ironic part is that moments like this have actually been (alongside other things) one of the reasons other women have left me. One past dumping, probably because we just weren't a match and too young to understand the complexities of a relationship, came about because of my own paranoia around being dumped. And this dumping has gone on to hold me back in other relationships since. If you don't laugh, you'll cry.

Anyone who has been through a breakup has likely felt some kind of trauma, and this might have caused you to act differently in future relationships. You pretend to be someone else, to act in a way that is less likely to cause the breakdown of the relationship or to make you repeat the traumatic event, but in doing so, you are not being your true self and I can

ENGAGE WITH PAST TRAUMA

guarantee trying to be someone else almost always fails, the mask always slips.

In an article in the *Huffington Post*, when discussing the issues with hiding your true self, Mary Morrissey put it like this: 'Pretending to be someone other than who you are only broadens the distance between yourself and the person you're trying to establish closeness with . . . Just keep in mind that you don't always have to hide that this is how you feel. You build REAL closeness with others through showing your true self, sharing your vulnerabilities and communicating how you really feel about things.'

Pretending to be anything other than your true self, especially because you fear being hurt again, will ironically more than likely cause you to get hurt again.

You may have even seen this in other people: they seemed so perfect and then, either suddenly or over a period of time, you see their true colours shining through. Yep, that's right – another three months you'll never get back. If you are deciding to date, it's always best to be as authentic as you can. There are so many possible partners out there that what one person dislikes can be another person's reason for infatuation. Welcome to the balance of the universe! Someone will fall for you, the *real* you, and they're much more likely to do so if you're presenting yourself honestly.

To continue using dating as an example, what some people can decide to do after being hurt is never to get into another relationship again. The pain of a breakup can be so much that people look to protect themselves against that. And I get it.

After all, why would you want to risk that again? While it is incredibly important to take time out at the end of a relationship, it's much better to evaluate what went wrong, what they did and what you did, rather than the unhealthy answer of putting up an impenetrable wall.

You can learn so much from experience, and a failed relationship is just that . . . experience. And a chance to grow. Just blocking out the pain instead of learning and progressing will cause you to repeat mistakes, waste time and fail again. You can tell yourself no, never again and then (because attraction is a funny thing and can come at any time), at some point, you meet someone, and that person that could be different, the one that you could actually make the exception for. But because you hid, instead of allowing yourself to learn and experience life, you're not ready for them. Your trauma is a wave, and you are the ocean: understand it, feel it, ride it and power on.

This same example works for any hurdle that you know you want to get over, but feel like you can't because of your past trauma. If you've experienced life-changing trauma then, in its aftermath, there's a high chance you may lack the ability to love yourself. Many can misinterpret pain as failure, whether from the choices you made or the fact that your life is not what you want it to be, and this can lead to feelings of worthlessness.

When we perceive that we've failed in anything, self-doubt naturally occurs. I applied for a job I wanted when I was 20; I was desperate to get it, it had great hours, great perks and was near to where I lived at the time. I was sure I'd get it. I thought

ENGAGE WITH PAST TRAUMA

I was perfect for the role; I studied the company and learned everything that I could about them. They told me no, and I was broken. The first thing I did was ask myself 'what's wrong with me?', and it sent me into a spiral of wondering whether I was just not up to it, whether I should rethink my career path and whether I was just not good enough. The proof of all that, in big bold letters, read: 'Thank you for applying, but we've decided to go in another direction.' This made my head spin, and I gave in. I decided to cancel the other interviews I had lined up. I figured I was just going to give up altogether, be a bum and mooch off my mum. The trauma of rejection had got to me, *big time.*

Luckily, my mum has a better head on her shoulders and probably panicked over the idea of having one of her adult sons still relying on her, and so she gave me the kick I needed. She explained that, regardless of what my preconceived thoughts about getting the job were, sometimes it's just not right, it's not a match, but that didn't mean that I wasn't the perfect candidate for a similar role in another company. She put me on a path that allowed me to learn from the experience, understand the process better and correct my mistakes.

Now, I never let negative experiences stop me. This is because, in my own traumatic childhood, there was a woman experiencing the same trauma and she managed to rise past it, move on from that marriage and create her own incredible life. Only a person who has gained strength from her own trauma could have helped me in those early years. It would, in the end, make me a stronger applicant and person. I went on to apply for five similar roles in other companies, being rejected a further four times but finally getting the 'yes' on the fifth.

I admire people who understand they've had a real sh*t time of it and continue regardless. I was lucky, in that I had my mum to keep me accountable, and I do understand we can't always have accountability buddies (more on this later), but I hope that, through this chapter and this book, I can give you the courage to keep going regardless of your past traumas. Because everyone's experience is unique, failure is subjective and bad experiences should never define you.

You're too comfortable with your trauma

So far in your life you have succumbed to the trauma and it has stopped you. This is nothing to be ashamed of, as we all do it. We use our trauma as crutches and whenever we struggle to get what we want, we use our past experiences as excuses. Your experiences of trauma have been filling your head with lies, lies that you are not worthy of your dreams or that you are unable to achieve them. That people like you don't deserve the cream. But it's time we stop listening to this irrational voice, do the opposite and use the trauma to make us take the first steps.

According to Psych Central, an organisation that promotes positive mental health and wellbeing news, one hurdle in overcoming trauma is that it is not physically held in the muscles or bones. Instead, the need to protect oneself from perceived

ENGAGE WITH PAST TRAUMA

threats is stored in the memory and the emotional centres of the brain, such as the hippocampus and amygdala. This activates the body whenever a situation reminds the person of the traumatic event.

For example, any time you think about asking someone out, you might shut down and make an excuse not to, because the mere thought of it reminds you of another traumatic experience of rejection you've had. The memory brings back the pain you felt, and your brain tries to avoid it at all costs. And, subsequently, we develop a similar comfort zone to help protect us from all kinds of trauma. Like many people in my early twenties, from time to time I would see a girl I found attractive, or even someone that I thought looked interesting, and I'd want to talk to them and get to know them. I thought I could develop a fun new chapter in my life, because connections can take us in all sorts of amazing directions. But then my muscle memory would kick in . . . 'It hurts to get rejected and they'd definitely reject me. Look at them! I bet they can just tell I've been rejected before and I can't experience another ego hit. I don't want that pain. It's fine, I'll leave it. She wasn't that pretty or as cool as she looked.' Cue dropping my head and starting to scroll on my phone. Any reminder of my trauma has been avoided, but, at the same time, I have missed out on a potential new experience and even a new relationship with someone I was excited to speak to.

My brain continues protecting me, saying things like: 'Ooh, it's so nice in this comfort zone – nothing can hurt me, if I stay right here and make sure I don't make any waves. If I do that,

I'll never get rejected again, I'll never make anyone disappointed in me, I'll never lose anything if I never have anything to start with. I'll just protect myself from anything that can hurt me.' This might seem like a great idea at first, but I promise you, it gets lonely and boring *very* fast. And, in the end, you'll end up disappointing yourself.

We let trauma stop us because it's easier to live in the comfort zone. The problem with comfort zones is nothing else other than avoidance gets accomplished from inside it. We don't go on to be captains of industry from the comfort zone; we don't go on to find the love of our lives from the comfort zone. At some point you'll realise you want to be remembered for something, but nothing will be remembered – you won't have accomplished anything because all you have done is avoid. It's time to stop protecting yourself.

Your life will begin on the other side of fear. Your fear of the trauma is holding you back. And we need to change your relationship with fear. To do this we are going to face the trauma and engage with it.

Talk to your trauma

I know it's going to hurt, and this part of self-development is definitely one of the toughest stages, but engaging with our trauma is a necessity. While we will discuss physical and mental practices away from the trauma to help us heal and recover, a big

ENGAGE WITH PAST TRAUMA

part of taking your life back is staring down and taking on the fear that is so deeply rooted within us. Because we could do all the other work, feel great about our life and then one thing can come along and trigger that memory all over again. Firstly, that will undo all of your brilliant progress and secondly, I will feel like I have failed you. So, lets dive into this important work . . .

To begin with, we need to understand what the trauma you are experiencing is. Is it a constant fear of rejection because of previous rejections, in recent memory or as a child? Is it fear of disappointing people in your life because of a hold they have on you? Has it come from experiencing something so truly traumatic that it has left you with a sense of worthlessness? The list of possible things that can hold you back through fear are endless. And while we can all try to avoid the source of our pain, I'm confident that you probably already know what is holding you back. If you are genuinely struggling to find the source, and you have a fear of progressing but don't know what holds you back, then I recommend some form of counselling or therapy (I will expand on the benefits of these later).

But for those who are able to pinpoint the issue at play and the cause of our stagnation, we need to learn what triggers our strongest reactions, not necessarily to be able to avoid them but to be prepared for when they crop up again. For me, growing up in an abusive home has made me especially sensitive, more sensitive than most, to signs of aggression and violence. I know that if I am yelled at, while it is situation dependent, I will almost certainly withdraw and become quiet. If I see violence in public or videos, it makes me uncomfortable and upset.

Once we know what these triggers are, what we are going to do with them is to develop a grounding routine. While there are different types of triggers, they all share one thing in common: they are all going to cause a strong emotional reaction, because they touch on your trauma. A grounding routine will help you stand tall and avoid having the wind knocked out of you when they make an appearance.

We will start by taking notice of how we feel about facing this trauma. Labelling an emotion as we feel it goes a long way to taking away its power. Are you feeling anxious? Are you overwhelmed? Are you able to calm down? Or has that boat sailed and all you feel is rage?

Now, label that, explaining to yourself what you're feeling as you think about facing that trigger, i.e. 'I'm now feeling nervous and anxious about the thought of putting myself out there and getting rejected.'

Next, question it as much as possible. Ask yourself questions like 'But is that internal outcome guaranteed?' and 'If it were to happen, why would it be so bad that it stops you from even trying?' And finally, ask yourself: 'What could you gain from facing this fear?'

Next, reposition by telling yourself that this fear can't hurt you. You can either have success with it or experience to gain from engaging with this trauma. Change your body language to that of a more confident stance (I will discuss confident body language in a later chapter) and take some deep breaths. Taking a deep breath while counting to five for each inhalation and exhalation can instantly help you relax and allow you to

ENGAGE WITH PAST TRAUMA

observe the emotion and the trigger without getting worked up. After following all these steps, you are ready to go.

UCLA's Matthew Lieberman refers to this process as 'affect labelling', and his research using MRI brain scans shows that this approach appears to decrease activity in the brain's emotional centres, including the amygdala. This dampening of our emotional brain allows its frontal lobe (the reasoning and thinking centre) to have greater sway over solving the problem or addressing fear.

Now that we have taken some power out of the trigger, we are going to face that trauma and fear and take it on.

Exposure therapy

NB: I want to note that this process depends very much on what kind of trauma you are trying to move past and in what way you're looking to beat it. If you're dealing with a lack of confidence in achieving something or you're scared of failing and rejection, then we will use techniques like exposure therapy, which have been proven to help. However, these won't work for all forms of trauma. For instance, as discussed, my childhood has made me very uncomfortable with acts of aggression, but I'm not going to purposefully seek out aggression to see how I hold up as that's not safe, nor is it healthy. Different traumas do need different responses, and, again, I recommend people go to licensed experts for any advice related to this, but, in addition to any professional help you receive, let me arm you with an attack plan for many of the triggers that can come up and which can cause some traumas to hold you back.

I sensed you squirm a little when I mentioned 'exposure therapy', but I promise you it is by far one of the best ways to master anything, and we are learning to master our destiny here, so I'm afraid this process is going to take a little bit of courage. Regardless of the trauma that caused it, exposure therapy is the most effective antidote for many past traumas. As an example, let's look at social anxiety.

Dr Karmen Smith, LCSW, DD, wrote this regarding exposure therapy for anxiety in an article on Talkspace.com: 'Exposure therapy for social anxiety is an evidence-based approach that helps those who struggle with the overwhelming fear and distress they experience in social settings. It can help them feel safe and confident when navigating certain social situations, like public speaking or meeting new people.'

Pushing yourself to constantly do the thing you most fear can disable the very same fear when you realise the outcome really is nothing like you imagined. Our anxious minds are a horrible judge of outcome. Not only do we prove ourselves wrong each time we speak to someone new, say, or go for something we didn't feel was attainable before, but, in repeating the action, we find it easier with each attempt.

For those who can drive a manual car ('stick' for the Americans among you), remember when you were first learning to drive how hard you had to concentrate when releasing the

ENGAGE WITH PAST TRAUMA

clutch from neutral. I honestly never thought I'd get the hang of it, and the effort seemed so infinitely hard to grasp, but you just keep doing it over and over again, and then one day you pull away in your car and you realise that you didn't think about it, that it just happened naturally. This is where we're going to get you to in relation to any area where you're currently anxious: the point where it's second nature and you're not even thinking about it anymore. In the case of social anxiety, we want to move from being barely able to string a sentence together when meeting a stranger to doing so without thinking. You can do it, you charming son of a gun!

Like I said, though, this is no easy ride and there will be peaks and troughs. The first few times you face your fears, the trauma will kick in, you'll remember exactly what the life experience felt like, the alarm bells will be blaring and the noise will be almost deafening. But you're going to ignore all the noise because it's *not real*, your brain has no proof that this experience will be the same as the last, and also because you have nothing to lose from trying. Many times I have pushed myself to do things that made me sweat bullets, but they always came before the act, not after. My mind was racing, and I felt sick, but the moment I was in the action, it all disappeared. In the beginning you'll be so immersed in the activity that you won't even know it's happened until after it's gone.

The thing that nobody tells you about confidence is that you generally aren't confident before the act, that confidence comes from *doing* it. Anyone you see who is confident in anything is that way because they have already done it. And repetition makes you a master.

Other tools

Like I've already said, however, we won't be using exposure therapy for all traumas. For the more extreme cases, I want to teach you how to handle the trauma to a point where something may remind you of it but you won't collapse in on yourself. You'll be at a point where you can stand and say, 'I am not going to let this affect me anymore, it's not going to hold me back from what I want in life.' We are not going to let it stop you from moving on with your life and accomplishing things your trauma never thought possible.

And we all need to start by talking about our traumas. I cannot express to you how good therapy is at uncovering and then healing your wounds. Personally, I believe anyone over the age of 25 should experience some kind of therapy. Not because everyone is mentally unwell, but because we can all too readily see what our parents and grandparents experienced by holding things in with a stiff upper lip, only to continue in pain. We also saw how they then projected their pain onto others, onto us, and how the cycle has continued.

I had CBT (Cognitive Behavioural Therapy) to help with high anxiety. CBT is a form of talking therapy that works by changing the way you think and behave, reprogramming your

ENGAGE WITH PAST TRAUMA

well-worn neural networks and introducing you to a fresh way of thinking. And it worked wonders for me. It gave me clarity as to why I was thinking in this anxious way and provided the tools to label it and question it (as we discussed before). I'm lucky to live in a country with free healthcare, so gaining access was relatively easy. But I know private therapy can be expensive, so while I still think it's worth it, because what you can achieve after receiving that kind of help will outweigh the cost, I do understand if you simply aren't in the position to get it. In that case, there are other options. Look online for what you're struggling with, either the trauma or the resulting condition, and look for support groups or free classes on handling them. There is also the option to just speak to someone you love and trust about it all, as the small act of offloading is likely to make you mentally lighter, but keep in mind that they are not trained professionals and so any advice they give is to be taken with a pinch of salt. But often, when we talk through these issues with others, we can see our own ways to help solve or deal with them, and I have found this can help a lot. You will gain strength from sharing. There are absolutely no benefits to keeping it all locked away. Even if you decide not to involve another person, and simply write your thoughts in a journal, this too can offer a similar release.

Much of this comes down to the importance of self-love. If you don't know what self-love is, I believe self-love (which we will discuss in greater detail in Chapter 8 – Build Self-Esteem Wherever Possible) is the act of doing right by yourself, it's looking after yourself physically and mentally. Eating the right foods, getting some form of exercise in as regularly as you can, having a good sleep routine and seeking out activities and hobbies that make you happy, including sports, art, music and meditation. All of these will contribute greatly to helping you let go of your trauma as any form of self-love proves to you that your experience is worthwhile and valid, and that you deserve a good life.

The Bridge to Recovery, an organisation dedicated to emotional recovery in the wake of trauma, says this in their article, 'Understanding Self-Love': 'When we experience trauma at any stage of our life, it violates our safety and often makes us question the things that make us, us. When trauma is left unresolved, there is a continued impact on our ability to love, and this can be detrimental. Self-Love is key to healing.'

Overall, treat yourself with the same kind of love you would someone else you love. Because when your brain starts to realise the good that is happening to you, and that you are worthy of this kind of love, you gain an extraordinary amount of self-confidence. Confidence that is not easily knocked off-kilter, even by past experiences. That is your way out.

Practise for self-love

A brilliant way to build self-love is to write down the attributes you possess that you like. Write down five to ten things and under each one, detail how you and others have benefited from them. This helps you to

ENGAGE WITH PAST TRAUMA

> take stock of the great things you currently do that might slip through the cracks. These things are more than likely built into you like second nature, so you may never realise the good they do. Start to take notice them more in your life and make a note of how you can honour these attributes more often. This will help you to build pride in yourself, leaving you more open to forgiveness of your past and giving you the strength to move beyond any trauma.

Letting go of trauma

While all of this should work and be useful for you, it won't just happen overnight. It's incredibly unlikely you're going to wake up tomorrow after reading this and feel that any fear related to your trauma has magically disappeared. However, because it has worked for me, and countless others I have spoken to in doing research for this book, I strongly believe this can work for you too. But two things are required. Firstly, you need to take action, and secondly, you need to be patient.

How long it takes for you to let go of your past traumatic experiences is different for everyone and dependent on how invested you are in doing so. It could take only a few days, it might take just a few months, or even years. This is not a race, though, and it's worth remembering that. You may start to feel much better and then the emotional 'muscle memory' may kick back in, and so the trauma rears its ugly head once more. But what I'm trying to share with you here is the idea that even if your trauma does come back, you now have a way of handling it. You may never completely let the pain of the past go, and that's okay, as long as you don't allow it to stop you. Just manage it in the best possible way as you experience it. And for the majority, doing what we've discussed in this chapter, as regularly as possible over a period of time, will set you on the path you've been craving.

Often after experiencing these momentous life events, we walk away with an overwhelming feeling of helplessness and we struggle to take back control of our lives afterwards. But overcoming the stress of your experience is often about taking action. In performing a positive action for yourself or those around you, you will start to take back control and reduce the feelings of helplessness. This can be any self-loving action, like getting into a healthy sleep cycle or eating right. You can even do small, positive actions for others, such as comforting a friend or helping someone who is struggling at work. Or you can go bigger by donating blood and volunteering your time for those less fortunate. Positive action will negate the negative, and by taking control of your life in this way, you will begin to feel good again.

Another incredibly positive thing you can do is to practise self-forgiveness. Our minds play cruel tricks on us by giving us examples of how we could have dealt with an experience better, but it's always after the fact. These actions, or this part of our brain, was nowhere to be seen during said experience and so ruminating on it is never going to be helpful. Your brain will tell you that you should have made this decision or said that thing or acted in this way, and then it would have been so different. So many times, after things haven't gone the way I hoped they would in a social interaction, I think, 'Why on earth didn't I say that witty remark that I'm thinking of now? Then it would have gone much better.' But that's not entirely accurate, and my mind has absolutely no proof as to whether being wittier would have stopped me from having an awkward encounter or meant that I dealt with the situation better. Your mind has no proof that, if you had done this, you would have had a different outcome. Yes, we can learn for next time, try different things to gain that proof, but until we do that, we cannot be sure, so instead we need to learn to forgive ourselves.

According to Spiral Psychology in an article by Dr Venetia Leonidaki on why self-forgiveness is hard but necessary, 'Self-forgiveness is the deliberate action to put behind us certain wrongdoings and let go of the pain linked to them. Self-forgiveness is neither about self-indulgence nor turning a blind eye to past mistakes. Instead, it requires courage to acknowledge these errors, take responsibility, and learn from them.'

To move on from any event we need to get the record straight. It happened and now there's not a damn thing you can do about it. You have experienced something that potentially you had no control over. It doesn't matter how many times you turn it over in your head as nothing would have changed that outcome. And even if you did have control or it was your own mistake, the moment has gone. We all make mistakes; I make them on an hourly basis! You must avoid being self-critical. Acknowledge that you made the mistake, but be okay about it. Imagine that the same thing happened to someone else you like – how would you treat them? You'd reassure them, right? Treat them with kindness and compassion? This is what you need to do for yourself. It's okay. It could have happened to anyone, and now you want better for your future, and you will have better, as that's why you're reading this book.

Forgive yourself because no one else is going to do it. You must move on for your own good, for your future.

Will it end?

I mentioned how my own traumatic life experiences have actually helped me in life. Yes, for most of my twenties, I allowed them to hold me back – I was enjoying my comfort zone, being lazy, being happy with the mediocre. But I was never truly happy and, like I said, it gets pretty boring and lonely like that. Instead, I admitted that I was lying to myself and wanted change. I worked out what was holding me back through research and therapy and then I tackled it all with the steps we've discussed in this chapter. Forcing myself out of my comfort zone and then learning from each experience was key. I still get pangs and reminders of my trauma, but now I handle them better. And the best part about it all is I

ENGAGE WITH PAST TRAUMA

don't shy away from traumas – I share them, I expose them. I use them to make things better for others now, through my content and now, through this book. Helping others to understand what holds them back and how to release themselves is incredibly rewarding and even helps me handle fear. So it may not completely end, but it *will* get better.

Hopefully, you've now learned how to engage with your trauma, by labelling it and exposing it. Taking away its power and then facing it on a regular basis. Each further chapter will help you on this journey, but at least now you have the tools to stop your past from having a say in your future.

> **Don't forget to share**
>
> Once you've worked out how to engage with and face your traumas, I want you to share them however you see fit. Find a way to help others through what you've experienced. Because that is an incredible way to live with trauma. Showing it who is in control, and now you can really work on what your life *after* trauma looks like. And helping people along the way is one of the best things you can do.

3
GET OVER YOURSELF

Understanding ego

You may or may not have realised through your own life, but throughout all our lives, our egos often control many of our thoughts, feelings and actions. Sometimes this is helpful. For example, our egos can help towards building a sense of self-worth and can also help us to build boundaries with others, by protecting our sense of what is right for us. However, in many cases our egos can be a hindrance and make us say and do things that we don't necessarily want to, and they also tend not to help towards us building an exciting successful life for ourselves, by equally stopping us from making decisions that might benefit us.

So, what is the ego? At a basic level our ego is our own sense of self-worth. On this level the ego doesn't sound like a bad thing, because having self-worth is a good thing. The trouble arises when we have an inflated or big ego, which leads to people thinking too highly of themselves, and this can have quite a damaging effect on our lives. The ego doesn't want to be seen in a bad light – it is powerful, controlling and can make you avoid things, such as when there is something you've always wanted to do (like starting a business or quitting your job), but the ego fears the way you will be perceived when attempting that goal or how it would look if you were to fail, so holds you back.

The ego can be incredibly self-conscious and can often be the reason we do certain things: the reason we wear certain clothes, the reason we express ourselves the way we do, the reason we present ourselves in certain ways at certain moments. It wants to be seen in a positive light and so is driven by external approval. It is based in fear, fear of how we are perceived, and it acts on those feelings by avoiding or showing off. But this is neither a productive nor a fulfilling way to live our lives, so let's get into how we can understand all this better and then refocus our ego for good.

> 'Ego will always want to come first, you have to control it and become its commander, only when you do this will you see your life truly improve.'
>
> UNKNOWN

In Chinese history there was a renowned philosopher named Wang Yangming. He created 'Xinxue', which translates as 'Heart Study'. One of its key teachings is that 'ego is the biggest enemy'. He goes on to describe how, when a person has an ego, every aspect of their life can go in the wrong direction: health, relationships and finances, all of these can be affected by your ego. Wang goes on to say: 'People become untrustworthy of other people who have big egos, because the ego can be very self-involved. Having a big ego can block your life beyond comprehension.' Wang Yangming could see the different ways that we let our egos affect us and I personally believe that the ego is to blame for a lot of unhappiness in modern life. We have all given our egos too much control and now we can't be carefree. Our decision-making is controlled by our ego, and we tend to shy away from doing anything that could potentially embarrass us, and this includes doing new things outside of our comfort zones, like starting a new business, asking out that person you like or trying a new hobby – the controlling ego can't allow us to fail or be seen to fail, so it won't allow us to attempt it. Our controlling ego can make us think it's a good idea to buy the flashiest car or designer handbag, so that we are seen and admired by others. Instead, we need to be making decisions for our self-improvement and not for the way they look to others. This is what I want to help you change. I want to get you to a point where you do not fear a damaged ego and go for what you want in life regardless. It's important to note that we do not want to completely destroy our ego, we just want to recalibrate it. Like I said before, self-worth is important; we just don't want the ego to grow so big that it gets in the way of our life – we want to use it for its strength and ignore it or control it when it becomes too inflated.

Dismantling your ego

The first step to recalibration is to understand that the ego is not *you*, it is actually separate from you. The tricky part is that the ego doesn't want you to think this way. It wants you to believe that it *is* you, but the ego is just a social mask, it is your self-image, how you want to display yourself to the world. It is *not* you – not the you when you're alone, when no one is watching. The social mask (ego) thrives on approval, and it is born out of fear. One benefit of the ego is that it can keep us going, motivating us to get up and attempt whatever we need to in life. But we are going to reshape it to do this not for approval of others but approval of ourselves.

The ego can manifest in numerous ways and in numerous parts of your life . . . Any of these sound familiar?

- 'At least I've got more followers than her.'
- 'I'm glad I make more money than my friends. I'm more successful than them.'
- 'My girlfriend's way hotter than theirs.'
- 'No way I'm going to do that, I'll end up looking like an idiot.'
- 'My life is going so great right now.'

These are all examples of our ego at its worst. Refusing to be beaten or to accept reality. Your ego can be ignorant and even force you to lie to others and yourself. It wants you to be seen as the best, with no blemishes. It can't take the truth that you are not perfect and never will be. Your ego is at its strongest when in public around others or when thinking about others (comparing you to others and what others will think of you). It feeds off approval and wants to be seen in a certain way (for example, the generous guy who buys dinner for his friends, or the successful girl who just got a promotion). Whatever the label is, it must be plastered across your head and everyone must know. And this can make you feel good, but there are a few reasons this way of thinking is hindering you.

Being so engrossed in how people see us is exhausting and unfulfilling, because nobody cares – everyone else is so wrapped up in their own stuff or projecting their own label, so nobody really cares if you make the most money, for example. The thought may occupy them for a few seconds at most, but then they forget about it. And because they forget, you never get the admiration that your ego is craving, meaning you never stop searching for admiration and you keep looking for new ways to gain the attention your ego requires. This is what I mean when I say that all this leads to a frustrating life of accomplishments that mean very little to you and your soul. We ignore areas of our life that may genuinely need improving, small things here or there that can improve our life significantly, becoming blind to the required improvement because that would mean admitting something is wrong. And your ego can't allow for that.

This also makes us inauthentic, as people cannot get close to us because our egos won't let others see us as human – and that means friendships or relationships never last long. You can't experience fulfilling connections unless you share your truth.

Your ego acts as a roadblock to anything that can make you look foolish or like a failure. This stunts your growth in achieving anything that is not expected of you. The idea that you could attempt and fail or even attempt and achieve anything that people you care about wouldn't expect you to do is a no go. The ego wants to protect this idealised image of you. For example, the ego may have labelled you as a successful student on the path to becoming the doctor you are expected to be. It cannot let you pack that in for a dream of becoming a fashion designer. 'What would people think? My parents would think I'm crazy, my friends would laugh at me, and what if I don't achieve it? I'll be judged. What a stupid thought . . . I'll just continue my studies. I'm going to be a doctor as that's what's expected from me, and then they will all be proud of me.' This is a common thought process for anyone who wants to do something outside of the box – the process of allowing your ego to talk you out of something is very similar for us all. The ego wants to keep us in the box and, in the end, we become disjointed. You must go for what *you* want, not what your ego wants. You have to be able to risk judgement (which is usually minimal anyway) and, even if people do judge you, this is usually forgotten quickly when they see how happy and content you are when you start following your own path, one meant for you, one without the desire for admiration.

GET OVER YOURSELF

For these reasons, you must refocus your ego and change the way your ego motivates you. To do that, we need to start by catching it, we need to catch it during the self-doubting loops and dialogue. 'I can't do this because others will judge', for example. You need to question this negative egotistical thought. Do so by reminding yourself that this is very unlikely to happen in the first instance, but if you *are* judged, remind yourself that this is your life you are living and not the life of those judging you. A helpful thought to keep close is to tell yourself that most people judge others because of jealousy and fear. Jealousy because they wish they could break free of their comfort zone and fear that, if you accomplish this, you'll leave them behind. Let them think this way; do not try and convince them otherwise and definitely do not put off attempting because of these haters' mindsets. This is for you and no one else. You'll never be hated on by someone doing better than you. Remember that.

Once you have practised this way of thinking, you need to question your own motivations, pause and rethink why you want to achieve this dream or goal. Are you doing this for the ego? To be better than everyone else? Are you doing it because you genuinely want this for you? For your happiness, regardless of what others will think or the outcome?

Finally, you need to restrict the ego from the goal or dream you are looking to accomplish. You need to

> detach from your thoughts or action to stop the ego getting too involved. You do this by changing the way you express yourself; instead of this being *your* goal, this is *a* goal you're attempting. Write down all the things you want to do and achieve, but underneath each goal write a note to yourself explaining how it would be great to achieve this, but that it is not the be-all and end-all. Write about how proud you are for yourself in attempting the task and how your world will still carry on if it doesn't work out, but that you owe it to yourself to try for a consistent period. If you don't want to write it, then just repeat it to yourself until you're convinced of this message. This helps create separation to ensure you don't become your goals. Remind yourself that you are just an individual who is attempting something.

This exercise is a great way to stop the ego becoming obsessed with the image and result because as we said before, as soon as the ego becomes too attached then we start second-guessing ourselves and making insecure decisions. Remember your timeline, tell yourself you're on your path and that the desired result will come, and that allowing the ego too much mental space will slow it down or even stop you from achieving your dream.

GET OVER YOURSELF

How to handle fear

In my opinion, fear is the single greatest stumbling block for anyone wanting to attempt something new or different. Fear has stopped literally millions of people from bettering themselves. Most people are not happy with a sub-par life experience but will never do anything about it because they have a voice in their head filling them with hypothetical and unlikely examples of how it could all go horribly wrong if they tried. So, they don't. They tell themselves that it is safer to just keep the status quo than be seen as a failure in anything. This is you, and this was me for a long time. But there is a difference between us and them. We want change, we *demand* change. You already started (and proved you're not just going to sit back) when you picked up this book. You are tipping the scales, and you've realised that the comfort zone is a far more dangerous place than putting yourself out there.

I used to talk myself out of doing all kinds of things. The excuses I told myself meshed perfectly with my anxious patterns of thinking and that's how I never really realised that I was putting these things off because of fear and was just plain scared. We do a fantastic job of lying to ourselves and protecting our ego. 'I'm not going to sign up for the gym, because it's too busy. I'll get in the way of people. Why should I pay for a gym when I can just get in shape at home? That's what I'll do, I'll just get some dumbbells and work out at home.' Of course, there are examples of people getting in great shape without stepping into a gym, but let's be honest: the simplest and most common way for them to do so is by exercising in a gym with the correct equipment. The monologue above is a real monologue that I told myself for years and years, despite wanting to get into better shape and really see what my body could do. And did I accomplish these from home workouts? No. I told myself lies for years just because I feared the gym and being judged. So much wasted energy on protecting myself (or my ego) and it got me nowhere.

And fear can materialise in many different ways – you may fear that you will simply just fail. You'll attempt something and it won't go well. So, if you never actually try, then you can tell yourself you could still do it one day, instead of *knowing* you can't.

Fear could be not wanting to be judged by people you know or even judged by complete strangers. You believe they could judge you for how you are attempting this goal, or you might be judged because it's not what people do in your circle, your family or your society.

We can handle our fears in multiple ways, but whatever the situation, we want to take back control of the fear, because at the moment the fear has control over you, it is physically stopping you from doing the task, goal or experience you want.

To take back control, I want you to break the fear down with three steps:

GET OVER YOURSELF

> Firstly, you need to think about the situation, the experience or goal you are attempting – write it down or hold it in your thoughts.
>
> Secondly, instead of thinking about the fear side of the situation, I want you to think about or write down something that actually makes you excited about the experience. This could be the outcome, the motivation or just something that will happen along the way. But it has to be something that genuinely makes you excited.
>
> Now the next and most important step is to bring that thought or image that makes you excited to the forefront of your mind and make this the anchor for your confidence. Write your anchor down, circle it, stick it on your mirror or fridge – anywhere you will see it often. This is now your own little tool that you can use against fear. Whenever you start hearing the voices expressing fear and why you shouldn't do this, remind yourself of your confidence anchor. You will do this from now on until that moment that whatever you are excited about happens. This is how you drop an anchor on those unwanted fears. The experience is never as bad as we think it will be, so follow your excitement and you're more likely to end up where you truly want to be.

Another tried and tested way for you to tackle fear is the 5 Second Rule. Invented by psychiatrist Mel Robbins, it's based on the idea that sometimes in life you just never feel like you are ready to do something, so you'll procrastinate and let the intrusive thoughts and fears win every time. You are just too scared, and therefore never ready to take that leap. The reason for this is that your brain is designed to protect you. Now, this is great if faced with real fear, i.e. real life-altering situations like a house fire, where you have to think about whether to go back in to save the family hamster. The fear of being burned alive will stop you from going into that house and so, in this instance, it is useful, but this thought process is not so helpful in less intense situations, like asking out your crush. You won't *die* if it goes badly, and arguably nothing bad will happen at all, but if you have an anxious mind, you'll be quick to highlight fears and overthink, yet it will probably never happen. But even if it doesn't go the way you want it to, doing any difficult task will at the very least have a lesson in it, so it's always worth doing.

In so many situations like this, a fear mindset is not welcome nor needed, and we really don't want our brain protecting us, so we need a bypass, which is the 5 Second Rule. The rule works like this: when faced with a scenario in which you are fearful of doing something, but that thing has no life-threatening aspect to you or anyone else involved, then you're going to count backwards from five and then do the task. Five, four, three, two, one, action. That's it. This is your jump-off point for any task that you're afraid to do and it's simple because it interrupts your current thought patterns of anxiety, fear, procrastination and overthinking. After counting down from five, your prefrontal cortex switches on, and this is the part of the brain you need if you want to learn something new or if you're taking some form of action. This will help you greatly when you feel frozen and undecided. And it will go a long way towards pausing the anxious thinking by not giving it any space to manoeuvre ... there's a countdown going off and you need to take action, so you haven't got time to work out how you will look or if other people will judge you. You just do it. It's a great way to handle the fear of judgement, and great for handling fear in general, but it's not the only way we can tackle this fear and, if the 5 Second Rule doesn't apply to you because the decision doesn't have to be immediate, then I also have some other techniques.

While I have already discussed in previous chapters how we fear being judged and how to stop this from affecting us, I will now give you an overarching way in which to get past or ignore the idea of being judged. This works especially well if you're unable to attempt the five-second exercise above, i.e. if you're not in an actual position to attempt the thing you're fearful about yet, because you're just thinking about it or you're not in the right physical location to attempt it. For this we can use the Are You Famous? rule. This is where you simply ask yourself, are you famous? If the answer is yes, well maybe people *are* judging you, as we have a strange obsession with famous people and love to judge any minor incidences or decisions they make. However, if the answer is no, then people aren't for the most part judging you – you might get a snap judgement made about you in the street based on your looks, behaviour or volume, but these judgements are quickly forgotten about by the passer-by and do not matter anyway, because we do not know them. As for the real-life changes, choices and decisions that we are talking about, (unless your famous) people generally aren't judging you. We need to put on our rational thinking cap and have a good ponder as to whether you will actually be judged if you attempt this new adventure. Are people really going to judge you in a negative light if you decide you no longer enjoy your nine-to-five and want something more for yourself? While you might think that Sandra on Facebook, who you haven't seen for 12 years, might judge you or be nosey about you, there's an incredibly high chance that she won't even notice, or forget about it within 30 seconds of finding out, because of the simple reason that nobody cares. Humans are far too wrapped up in their own nonsense to even notice what you do with your life. As a rule, this goes for Sandra or even your closest friends. There's a quote that has been attributed to Winston Churchill that goes 'When you're 20, you worry about what others think of you. When you're 40, you stop worrying. When you're 60, you realised nobody was thinking of you in the first place.'

No one is going to really judge you, in essence, unless you're famous.

And this feeds back to you as well: don't be too quick to judge others for their life choices. If you haven't already realised, life can be bloody hard sometimes and people do what they need to in order to survive.

However, there are some people who will judge and some that will get in the way, but it is always a good bet, when thinking 'what will so and so think?', to do whatever it is regardless. Remind yourself that you are living your life, that you only have the one and, when you're on your death bed, you won't be thinking 'I'm glad I didn't go for that job when I was younger because it would have annoyed my mum'. It's your life, and no one else gets to live it for you or tell you what to do with it.

Sometimes we believe that people will judge us within the industry or place we are in now for attempting this new change. One of the reasons I put off joining a gym for so long was the fear that I would be laughed at by the big muscle men of the gym as I was such a skinny rake, but this couldn't be further from the truth. I actually found that people were rooting for me, that they recognised their own journey in me, and it reminded them of their humble beginnings and so they were incredibly happy to help with any advice when asked. The same thing happens in new work environments or when you're attempting to create something from scratch. The experts who have done it before do not sit in their ivory towers judging the newcomers – no, they welcome them and are always happy to help, because they see themselves in you.

So, in order to move past it, a different mindset is needed when we fear taking new steps for fear of being judged. It's at this moment that we need to be more self-aware, instead of just letting the fearful thoughts run wild and claim another victory.

> To do this exercise I would recommend writing down the task or goal in the middle of a page and then we will create a spider diagram of our fears related to that goal around it. Let's say, for this example, that the fear is 'performing something in public'. Take two different colours and circle each fear accordingly, distinguishing between fears we can do something about (how well you perform, how well-rehearsed you are and whether you have the correct equipment, for example) and then fears and outcomes we have no control over (i.e. whether people actually like what you are performing, or whether you get booed).

Once we see the fears written down and out of our head, it's easier to question their validity and the hold they seem to have over us.

The fears we circled above that we can do something about are of our main focus from this point on, simply because we have control over them and we can work towards debunking the supposed fear or do something about them. For example, if you practice regularly and plan ahead, it's incredibly unlikely you'll get booed or have everyone not like your performance. Concentrate on what you *can* control and use this diagram to be aware of when you're putting yourself off doing something for fear of being judged.

GET OVER YOURSELF

The realisation of how much we control (wake up, you run this sh*t!)

> 'A reminder of how IN control you are – even when it feels the complete opposite.'
>
> UNKNOWN

It's a common thought process to place blame on others or circumstances. Many people experience these kinds of thoughts at some point. For example, 'I'm not happy with my life. I might be content, but I could definitely be happier. I feel like I was made for more, but what can I do? Great things don't happen to me, they happen to other people.' We focus on anything other than that we ourselves are the reason for our predicament. When we think this enough, and allow it to ruminate in our minds, it becomes easy to genuinely believe it. Our mind is easily swayed and before long it believes whatever you feed it. You may even feel completely helpless, but it is my mission to make you realise you are in control of everything and always have been.

Every day you wake up and *you* get to choose who you want to be. Today you do not need to be the person you have created; sure, you may have spent all your life up to this point building this version of yourself, the version that most people expect of you, but this could have been built on fear-based thinking and the need to make people like you. My hope is this book opens you up to a new way of thinking and a new life that you want to live. This can start right now and only you get to choose who you want to be. And to start that process, I have some reminders for you:

> *You* get to choose what you want to do.
> *You* also get to choose how you want to handle things.
> *You* control how people perceive you.
> *You* control your thoughts.
> *You* control your perspective.
> *You* control how you treat yourself.
> *You* are in control of your happiness.
> *You* control how much time you waste worrying.
> *You* control what you want to do today.
> And, finally, *you* control who you want to become.

Nobody and nothing are here to stop you. There is nothing fighting against you because *you* have the ability to think and feel and watch what happens. When you realise that it has always been you *vs* you, you can finally grow. You can get out of your own way.

Letting go of societal expectations

Depending on where you were born or live, there are different societal expectations placed upon us. These are also known as societal pressures and they will have been affecting you most of your life, whether you know it or not. These expectations can come through family (i.e. find a good job, get married and have kids), media (i.e. what things you should consume and like) and education (i.e. follow the standard educational path of school, college and university). While the good side to these expectations is it gives your life some order, direction and helps you fit in, the bad side is there's a high chance it can push you in the wrong direction and convince you to make life decisions that others prefer instead of what you actually want. We tend to want to conform to the masses and we don't want to stand out, because, as discussed earlier in this chapter, we can fear being judged for our choices and actions, and the people we fear seeing us in a negative light are those close to us – friends, families, communities. Sometimes we fear that standing out and being different to these people will lead to us being shunned, turned away or not accepted, and this is where our surroundings and our societies can stunt us.

You may want to attempt something that is unheard of in your society. You may have outspoken people in your life that think you should only work on becoming an engineer, say, but you don't want to do that, and instead you want to be an animator. However, because of societal pressure, you conform. You may even be a people pleaser, so you never attempt your dream and you become an engineer because that's what your society expected of you. This, of course, over a long period of time leads to unhappiness and a sense of being unfulfilled.

It can also work in the opposite direction. Maybe your

societal pressure is from the friends you hang around with? You may be very close because you've grown up with them, but all they enjoy is lazing about, but you want to do things differently – you want more. You want to get up off your butt and do something real with your life, but that might mean losing these friends. Either way we tend to just conform because it's easier, and the idea of being judged by them in our head is awful.

According to Better Help, the mental health platform, in their article about how social pressures impact on us, they researched one study using brain scans that found: 'social pressure and the responses it elicits seem to have measurable effects on the brain. It can therefore be possible that social pressure might potentially alter a person's perception of reality in some way, since it can lead to detectable changes in the brain itself.' The study goes on to say: 'Humans also tend to look at the groups we're in for guidance about what to do and how to behave. In psychology, this is known as the "principle of social proof".'

I believe that social proof can be thought of as subtle social pressure. When we make decisions based on social proof, we may assume that this is the best course of action because a lot of people do the activity or like whatever it is. And following the crowd helps you to fit in, it helps build friendships and relationships, but it doesn't help you when your dreams or goals are not aligned with your society's values. Plus, it takes great strength to go against the grain, so how do you do that?

Well, you're going to have to grit your teeth and move

GET OVER YOURSELF

forward regardless, because this is all about doing what's best for you and not holding back on account of our societies, families and friends.

> You will have to start by embracing your individualism. I advise you to question yourself: Who are you? What are your attributes? What are your interests, your values, and what feelings make up *you*? Write them down. Live by what you have written down and make life decisions that enhance these statements. I'm asking you to be vulnerable and to be as authentic as you can, and when you do this, and are aware of these life markers, you can also be aware of when you are hiding from them or minimising them because of other people or societal pressures. It's at this point that you must go against the grain and embrace who you are and what you want.

It shouldn't matter if this is not the norm for someone with your background – you will have to become proud of what you're doing and believe you are not only going in the right direction but also inspiring others to break out of their own fear bubbles. Your individualism can have a positive effect on not just you but society as a whole, inspiring others to broaden their outlook. You grow and we all grow.

I would also recommend seeking support from someone or a group that has either done something similar by going against the grain or people related to what it is you're trying to achieve, to help build your confidence in achieving your goal and understanding of the process. You can do this by reaching out to people on social media who might have similar backgrounds to you that have achieved something not expected of them.

And, lastly, measure your progress by your *own* measuring stick and not others'. Set clear goals from the start and then set aside time to celebrate your success as you mark off your achievements. These can be big or small – it doesn't matter as the point is that you get to decide what is a goal and what is an achievement.

How to handle social media and avoid an addiction to it

Another place that might be outside of your society and communities but still hold you back from expressing individualism is social media. How we look at social media and how we use it can act as a block to us being proud to express ourselves and try new things. Individualism is what makes you great and it is your single biggest weapon against conforming. Most people are the same: we eat the same foods, buy the same clothes, do the same things. Social media shows us what everyone else is doing, and we get FOMO (fear of missing out), leading to us and everyone else wanting to do and experience the same things. This happens to all of us. I have quite a few items of clothing that I've bought because I saw people online in them, and many people go on holiday to the same places because they've seen people (influencers) holidaying there. But this conformity is so destructive to your happiness, because while you are making your own decisions, you are doing so blind, believing this is what you want because someone else has said it is . . . and now you are living someone else's life. People have an addiction to fitting in.

The *Huffington Post* posted an article by Sally Biddall on their website entitled 'Is Social Media Turning Us Into Clones?' The argument of the article is summed up well: 'It's natural for us to want to be part of something, whether that's a community in the physical sense or, more recently, online. However, I do think there's a danger of us slowly losing our individuality [with social media]. Our little quirks and idiosyncrasies are what make us unique after all.' The piece then goes on to discuss how many Instagram users are following each other's interests and styles, and can remove the beauty of individuality.

You've probably experienced it yourself, whether deciding on certain style choices, wanting to go to certain locations or mirror certain lifestyles. There's been a few times when I've even thought about cutting a slight mullet into my hair because I've seen the cut so many times across social media . . .

So, a different mindset is needed to avoid all this on social media and any other media you consume. Just because we see a lot of people dressed a certain way or in certain brands doesn't mean we need to do the same to be accepted. What you wear or what Stanley cup you drink from (I also have a Stanley, that said) will never be the defining reason you have strong relationships and friendships as this will come down to your personality. So, when you want to express yourself on social media or otherwise, do so with your own ideas and interests. It's better to be an outlier than a clone.

You can only do this by venturing into the unknown, however; by trying things you've never done before, wearing certain styles because you genuinely enjoy and like them and not because they're the latest thing. Add new layers and dimensions to your character by going to places you never would have before, purely because you think they're interesting and not because they're the top destination that year; even simply by experiencing something new outside of your comfort zone – a cooking class or a dance class, say. Force yourself to think outside of your box and let go of any labels you or anyone else have placed on you. Bring new ingredients into the mix, audit your old thought patterns, and reflect on your new experiences. This is such an import step in becoming exceptional – you do not create meaning in your life, you discover it. And you do this through experimentation and pushing past what your society expects of you. Your true potential isn't someone else's path.

So, with this adjusted mindset, when you look through the lenses of social media and see others living their lives, you will not be thinking you're missing out as you won't be using it to follow trends, or mimic anyone else. Others are posting whatever they want, but that's their path and you are on your own path, and whether you want to share that with social media is up to you as you won't be doing it to show off, just to keep close ones updated with your journey. You are not missing anything, because the only thing that matters is what you do with your life. Keep this in mind if you catch yourself looking at someone else living the life you think you want on social media. Why do you think that is what you want? That that is what your life should be?

Maybe you think that's the life you deserve. Here is a hard truth: you don't deserve it. And you don't want it. Not that badly anyway. Because if you truly wanted it that badly, you would have it, and you would have already worked your butt off to achieve that life. You would have put yourself in a position to attain it; you would have made the moves towards this life. But you haven't (yet) and this is why you don't deserve it. This leaves us two options: acceptance or change.

Social media has done a brilliant job of connecting people, demonstrating different cultures, ways of sharing interests and showing us possibilities. But we take that for granted now as the internet has been around long enough that it's just part of our day to day, so what most of us use it for now is shopping and comparing. Regular reminders of what else you could have, and then you become addicted to the daydream . . . you've become addicted to escaping.

While this feels nice in the moment – imagining your life in a different setting with many new and shiny things – reality hits pretty quick and pretty hard. You *don't* have those things and your life is *not* like this. Now you're sad, pissed off at your life, and depressed. Then you pick up your phone and repeat the process.

So, the answer to this is acceptance or change. You accept that what you have is your life for now, but it doesn't have to be forever. You accept that you really do want the change, and you want it badly enough to accept that, if you continue on your current path, you are never going to get it. You can use social media as a tool to push you towards something bigger and better than you ever thought possible. Too many just wish and never make the moves to change: for some they are too mentally weak to go for it. And then they have to accept it will never happen, which, by the way, is okay for them as long as they are happy to accept their lot in life. But they still need to change the way they look at social media as they can't keep looking at the what-ifs. You should remove anything from your social media that makes you jealous since the effect on your mental health is too much and is really not worth it. Unless, that is, you use it for motivation to actually do something about your life.

The dopamine you get from seeing things you like also stunts you. You don't feel the need to go out and experience the things you see because you are getting a form of enjoyment from just seeing them. You suddenly have no motivation to achieve and instead have the things you like on social media, because you already get what you want from it. Or you feel so crappy about yourself because you don't have what you see and then all the motivation is sucked out of you.

You need to reframe the way you use social media, sure, but maybe go further and delete any accounts or apps that genuinely put you in a funk? You want your life to be a positive one. You want your mind to be filled with positive thoughts, and if aspects of social media are doing the opposite, then they need to go. No more looking at accounts of people overselling their lives because what they are producing is mostly fabricated and created for likes and follows. Everyone struggles and everyone creates negative thoughts. Be better than them by ignoring them and creating something that you are truly content with. A life you are proud of and don't want to compare with others. Only *you* get to decide what you want. So, make the move to achieve it but learn to enjoy all of it, because even when you achieve the life you covet, there will be something else or someone else for you to compare yourself to. The faster you can quit comparing and start enjoying, the faster you'll actually be content.

Letting go of previous versions of yourself

Pivotal moments happen, and most likely already have happened in your life, all of which build and shape who you are. We are crafted out of our most difficult moments. How we handle the big stuff determines who we are. Labels and titles are created, and the way you are with people around you will do this – for example, constantly making jokes with friends might give you the label of being the clown, or being the family member who always sorts out the family issues will have you labelled as the peacemaker. This is a double-edged sword.

We all have difficult moments in our childhood and how we

handled them can impact how we feel about ourselves now. On the one hand, you could have handled these moments by being brave, at which point you became a leader in your home and with your friends. You could also have handled those difficult moments through humour and now you are seen as the joker.

This latter one was me. I'm not talking about the DC Comics' version of The Joker, I mean the person who uses humour to deal with uncomfortable moments. By attacking the problem with humour, I made one or two people laugh and diffused the tension. I enjoyed how it made me feel as I was finally receiving some form of validation, but then I would run to always wanting to make people laugh, always wanting to be the funniest in the room, always there with the wittiest remark. However, chasing adulation with my quick wit led me nowhere, because when all you crave is other people finding you funny to cover up the cracks in your confidence, when you're on your own or when you don't have the laughter around, it does nothing for your self-esteem (I will discuss how to build your self-esteem in Chapter 8 – Build Self-Esteem Wherever Possible). These invisible labels we receive throughout our lives can become detrimental to our growth and overall experience of life. The labels are adopted by friends, peers, family and especially by you, because of the mask you have shown to those around you (bravery, humour, pessimism etc.) formed due to your life experiences, and if worn for too long, it becomes fully developed and a potentially permanent feature.

And not only do labels spread, they endure. I was seen as the comedian and, to some people, I still am. This becomes incredibly frustrating when I try to show any other side of myself other than the comedian aspect, such as a burgeoning career in self-improvement. Because it is not expected and people do not like to be surprised or wrong about someone, they try to keep that person in whatever box they know. Then you doubt yourself and question 'maybe this isn't me?'

Many of us are trying something new, something bold and scary, but, most importantly, something outside of our comfort zones. And as that's not where people close to you expect you to be, there's a high chance you'll meet resistance. You may discuss your plans or just start doing them and the people closest to you might tell you to be careful and act wary. They can make you feel like you're silly for changing or wanting change, but I am here to tell you that you *can* change, you are *not* your label, and it is time to push past the version of you that you believe yourself to be and the version of yourself that you have been projecting for years. You are more than a label, and you need not care if any change to the old label is met with resistance. Do not let this label define you.

Charles Darwin was once seen as the dumb one in his family. Dropping out of two colleges, his father and his masters considered him an average person with a below the common standard of intellect. He was chastised by his father for not applying himself properly. But Darwin didn't let this label define him, he considered himself bright and wanted to apply himself in another direction. Charles Darwin is now regarded as one of the most influential scientific minds ever to exist. His theories on natural selection and evolution have affected us all.

GET OUT OF YOUR OWN WAY

Your job is to shake off these labels, but mainly for yourself. You are now going to let go of any old versions of yourself that don't align with what you now want. No person is just one thing, and while those closest to you may always see you as a singular type of person, you can still surprise people with your multifaceted personality.

> Let's start by thinking about the different labels we have picked up over the years. Some of these labels you will know, but some you may not, so it might be helpful to ask those close to you to share the labels they have for you. Then, when you have them, write them down and consider if these align with the person you think you are and who you want to be. If they don't, then write down the labels you do want to live by, the ones you think do apply. Once you have that in your head and written down, you can live a life in accordance with the preferred labels, make life decisions based on what you believe someone of that label would do, showing the world you are a person of multiple skills and labels. Surprise everyone, yourself included, and do something nobody expected of you. It starts with the first step; make that step and you are already the change you desire.

GET OVER YOURSELF

You may think you're only good for one thing because those around you and society have told you so. It's easy to succumb to the notion that you can't be anything else, but you can, and at any point in your life too. You need to believe that you can still have a beautiful life for yourself.

The art of staying humble

When you find success in your life there will likely be pride attached to the result. You've worked hard and you're understandably proud of that. But what can happen when people are very successful is that their ego becomes inflated and they become arrogant – we've discussed the negatives of this already. So, what is the alternative? How should we be when we become successful?

Being a success and then lording it over others screams insecurity and low self-esteem. This is a 'small mindset' energy and there's no space for it on your journey. Instead, you will be better off with the mindset that's more 'I'm doing great, well done me, but I'm not finished, I still have continuous work to do on myself.' This is the art of staying humble.

> 'Humility is the ability to accurately view your talents and flaws while being void of arrogance. Some believe that being humble means having low self-esteem and a lack of confidence, but it's the opposite. Humility is having the self-esteem to understand that even though you are doing well, you do not have to brag or gloat about it.'
>
> TIARA BLAIN, VERYWELLMIND.COM

Humility helps build your self-awareness; it broadens your mindset and allows you to question 'where can I improve?' As we discussed in Chapter 1, your journey is never quite over, as you experience both your Overall Timeline and goals throughout your life, and you always have ways to expand and improve. Being humble gives you the space to do that. When you moved up a level in your life, you should congratulate yourself, but, at the same time, there may be many more levels you will want to climb, and being humble allows you to realise that you need to improve to get to the next level. If you act arrogant and think you're the best, then you'll end up staying on that level, either for ever or a lot longer than you need to.

Humility will also help you with your goal setting. If being humble helps you gain far better self-awareness, then that puts you in a much better position to understand your wants and needs. It allows you to go for what you want for your own sake, rather than building based upon the wants and wishes of others or ideas based on social proof.

It's important to understand that being humble doesn't mean

you shouldn't be proud. Pride is important, and it is definitely not a negative attribute, but there's a line to look out for. The real key is to use humility and pride in tandem. Do not allow pride to take centre stage without humility. This is where pride becomes extreme and shows itself through narcissistic and selfish behaviours. Being humble will help you in forming strong friendships and relationships. Someone who is self-aware is also aware of other people's feelings and emotions. Being empathetic and in tune with other people will help you greatly in building these solid relationships.

So how do we avoid too much pride and be humbler in our lives? Well, this whole chapter has been an example of how to be humble. We reframe the ego so we don't measure our success by external status symbols, like how much money we have or what position we're in. Leading on from that, you stop comparing your life to others. Everyone is going through life with the same highs and lows, and you cannot escape the rollercoaster either. Be willing to accept that none of us are perfect, yourself included – you have flaws, I have flaws, so find ways you'd like to improve, for yourself. Help others through your success, and share your knowledge and your story – we all love an open and honest person; we trust them, and you can become an incredible person, adored by the ones who matter most to you, by living with a humble mentality.

Handling 'Imposter syndrome'

'I'm an imposter.' This is a thought I've had to tackle on a regular basis. When you become successful in any field, after the high has worn off you start to question if you deserve it, if you deserve to be in this position. Just as when we were talking about incredible people earlier in the 'Design Your Own Timeline' chapter, we see these people who have done amazing things and then just assume they are incredible people for what they have achieved and believe they were probably always brilliant. But most of the time that is not the case. And I will bet you a pretty penny that the majority of these people have felt some level of Imposter syndrome as well.

Psychology Today states in an article on Imposter syndrome: 'People who struggle with Imposter syndrome believe that they are undeserving of their achievements and the high esteem in which they are, in fact, generally held. They feel that they aren't as competent or intelligent as others might think – and that soon enough, people will discover the truth about them.'

Albert Einstein would regularly pronounce himself a 'voluntary swindler'. He believed his work should never have received the adulation he experienced. For someone of such incredible success in his field to regularly self-doubt, it shows how easy it is for everyone else to do so.

You may have already experienced this feeling yourself; you may have achieved something and felt like there were other people more deserving. Imposter syndrome can make you feel

GET OVER YOURSELF

like a fraud, and even if you've worked your butt off to achieve something, someone with this syndrome will tend to accredit the success to luck, when instead they should be appreciating their capabilities and effort.

For me, I used to experience Imposter syndrome most when being praised for what I had achieved. I would rather shrug it off and say it was good timing than acknowledge how much effort I put in.

And a side to success that no one tends to talk about is that it comes with responsibility. Whether it's a work position or admiration for something you've done, you now have a new responsibility regarding that success. Your new job might carry responsibilities that you didn't think about when you were trying to succeed, or you may have created a name for yourself in your field and now many people look up to you and watch your every move.

You may have found rapid success in something and gained plaudits for your achievement, but this can definitely make you feel like an imposter because you might question, 'Why me?' Others have been working on this for years or a lifetime . . . why have *you* become an instant success and they haven't? However, I want you to know, if you find yourself in this situation, you do not need to have lived your whole life dedicated to one field to be successful in it. Any success, rapid or otherwise, will have hard work put into it, a love for the craft and persistence. Do not put yourself down by thinking you are unworthy, because you are definitely still deserving.

If you are inclined to think this way, you are actively stunting yourself, or at the very least, you'll be slowing yourself down. You aren't looking to take yourself to the next level because you're already thinking about how you're just lucky to be here anyway. I grew a very large social media following pretty quickly and I would look at the other struggling content creators and think, 'Oh, wow, their work is even better than mine and they haven't had the same success. I've just got lucky.' This stunted my work for almost a year. I suddenly found myself questioning everything. Basically, I completely got in my own way. Instead, I should have been focusing on everything I did to get myself in this position and looking to elevate my content to a new level instead of worrying that I was a fraud.

So, what did I do about it? I talked about it. I would regularly be told by my loved ones that these thoughts of fraudulence were unfounded. They reminded me of the graft I had put in to achieving this, but then they said something I wasn't expecting: they told me they themselves had also felt these feelings in their own field.

In comes 'pluralistic ignorance'. Pluralistic ignorance is where we each doubt ourselves privately but believe we are alone in thinking that way, especially as no one else talks about it. This is something that almost everyone experiences at some point in their life. And I opened a door for myself by talking about my own fears. Rejuvenated by this, I reached out to others in the content community and, lo and behold, so many of them, people I deemed more successful than me, had also been experiencing this same issue.

If you work towards achieving something, and you succeed in

your mission, then you deserve it. Hard work does pay off, but, equally, dreams can be achieved with less. Neither are more deserving as long as it was a conscious effort to accomplish something, followed by action. You went for it; you got it and now you deserve it. Do not waste time questioning what has happened, do your best to harness what got you there so that if you want to go bigger and better, then you can make the conscious effort in doing so. Just remember many incredible people just like you have experienced the same waves of doubt, but it never stopped them from being successful or achieving even greater success.

You *vs* you

There's an old saying that goes: 'When you grow up in a house that is burning, it is easy to think the whole world is burning too'. As we grew up, we have all put constraints on our lives by conforming with societal expectations and applying labels to ourselves. But the reality is that nothing has actual control over us. Often we place ourselves under this control and impose limits on ourselves. Sometimes we allow our ego and fear of being judged to come before anything else. We can be guilty of blaming others or circumstances for holding us back so far, but hopefully, with the help of this chapter, you can see that the culprit for our lack of growth is ourselves. So, we need to start catching ourselves in these ego-driven ways of thinking, question how much we care about how people perceive us and not allow our egos to become too attached to our dreams and goals.

You are going to experience this journey, but the journey isn't you. How you are perceived and what you experience are a reflection of the goal and not of you. You'll begin to break your fears apart, dissect them and expose their ridiculousness. Learn to gain control of your social media use and stop it from getting in the way of what you want by deleting or unfollowing anything that doesn't aid you in this journey. Question motives and catch the intrusive thoughts that weigh on your mind. Your life has never been about you *vs* other people, and you shouldn't give a f*ck about what others are doing with their lives. In fact, obsession with comparison is what stunts us the most. Take a look in the mirror: that person in the reflection is who will make or break your life, through your daily choices and how you manage your internal dialogue. It has always been you *vs* you. We have control over our own destiny, no one else. You have the power to make something incredible. Care less about what others think and care more about what you want to achieve.

4
GROW FROM FAILURE

Failure is necessary

> 'I don't know what your future is, but if you are willing to take the hard way, the more complicated one, the one with more failures at first than successes, the one that has ultimately proven to have more meaning, more victory, more glory, then you will not regret it.
>
> 'Whateverr you choose for a career path, remember the struggles along the way are only meant to shape you for your purpose.'
>
> CHADWICK BOSEMAN

Failure is necessary. It is not only a part of your journey, but *the* journey. We have to fail in order to succeed. It is simply not possible to be perfect on the first go. We might come out of the gates flying, but we will never be consistently perfect.

Whatever it is you are trying to accomplish, you are more than likely to fail more than you actually succeed. Failure is inherently part of being great so it is imperative that you not only get used to failing but you adopt it as an integral part of your life. Too many people run from failure, they run so far that they never even attempt it. If you're serious about creating the future that you want, then failure will become a key part of your life, and you will learn to be comfortable with that, because without it you do not succeed at any of this.

While discussing inventions, Thomas Edison's associate, Walter S. Mallory, said to him, 'Isn't it a shame that with the tremendous amount of work you have done, you haven't been able to get any results?' Edison replied, 'Results! Why, man, I have gotten a lot of results! I know several thousand things that won't work.' While said with an undercurrent of sarcasm, this is very much an important lesson as Edison made sure to learn from his non-starters and instead of giving up, he used them as motivation to find something that *did* work. His successful projects include but are not limited to the incandescent light bulb and the motion-picture camera.

What we need to learn is that failure is the teacher, and failure is the process. I have failed more than I have succeeded. I have created more videos on my social media with under 10,000 views than I have videos with over 100,000 views. Yes, 10,000 might seem like a lot to some, but for me it's not good enough. I take each failure, and I learn; I attempt to make my

GROW FROM FAILURE

content better. Sometimes that works and sometimes it does not. I do not, however, let that stop me from adapting and trying again. However defeating it sometimes feels, you must trust in yourself to keep creating, keep attempting, because one day one of your attempts could be incredibly successful. This process has allowed me to make numerous videos for my social media with over a million views and engagements. These are the videos I am remembered for, not the videos with under 10,000 views. These are the videos people will share and will talk about. These are the videos that have given me the opportunity to write this book. I could never have had any of that success if, at first, I had not failed and continued to handle failure.

There is nobody in this world or throughout time that gets it right every single time. Nobody is perfect. Be less harsh on yourself and keep that fact in mind: let it give you the confidence to try new things and go for your dreams. Your dreams are your dreams because you do not already possess them. They are ideals and goals that you want to accomplish but you do not have them yet. To obtain something you do not have, you have to do something you have never done. Failure is a part of any life and, if you don't fail, then maybe you need to push yourself a little further.

How to learn from each failure

You may have heard the term 'overnight success' before, but it sounds fairly self-explanatory: someone becomes incredibly successful in a very short amount of time, either overnight or within a few days. Statistically, this is very unlikely, because success takes time, failures, lessons and strategy. However, it doesn't stop most people believing they are capable of attempting something and then being successful very quickly, myself included. When I first started creating content, I naively thought it would grow quicker and that I would be successful faster. I learned my lesson before long, but it's natural for people to be impatient, shortcut-minded and bored, all of which have negative effects on effort and results. We must dispel this ideal that we need to become an overnight success, or that our goals need to be completed immediately. If something you strive for can be completed quickly, then great, but mostly, in life, the good stuff takes time. When Facebook's co-founder Dustin Moskovitz was asked in an interview about Facebook's success, how he felt about his seemingly rapid success, he said, 'If by overnight success you mean staying up and coding all night, every night for six years straight, then it felt quite tiring and stressful.' Rarely does anyone escape hard work on their path to success and Dustin would attest to this. A big part of that hard work is navigating and learning from setbacks, and there would have been plenty of setbacks and failures during those six years – these setbacks would have been integral to the success of Facebook.

GROW FROM FAILURE

Every time you fail you are one step closer: having this mindset allows you to embrace failure. By all means try your best, though. You have to put in some effort, so try your best and be accepting of the failure, because when you attempt your best, you allow yourself the space to learn instead of already knowing you could have just put in more effort. So, if you fail after working your butt off, ask yourself: what has this failed attempt taught me? What can I add or remove for next time?

Jamie Johnson of Business.com in an article about facing our failures puts it this way: 'When you encounter failure, tackle it head-on and learn from your mistakes. Realise that every idea that pops up in your mind isn't going to work. Take the time to organise your thoughts after a failure and realise what you did wrong. Above all else, be willing to learn and grow.'

Look for the pinpoints in your failure, take them in, dissect them and find the source. Take a moment to ask yourself why has this happened? Was it something you did or was it something external that contributed this time around? The majority of the time it will come down to something you did, even if it feels external, and you will still have had some element of control over that. Look for ways to be accountable and don't forget how much control you actually have. Blaming external factors is lazy; it is a self-serving bias and will keep you stuck in the same spot.

Most of the time, when we adapt what we have learned from the failure, it means that we need to offer up some sort of change. This change will be the answer to your success, or at least a more successful attempt. Understand what needs to change and do not shy away from making that change – this is the key to learning from our failures. Change can be difficult for some as we naturally like our routines or the people we hold close, but sometimes change means making a rift in that routine. While it's for the greater good, it can still be hard. We sometimes don't want to make the change that is needed because it can have a reverberating effect. For example, removing someone or something that is not needed: these people or things may have sentimental value. Or maybe you need to add something that is a financial expense and you will have to work out a way to afford it? I know this is easy for me to say from a distance, and without knowing your circumstances, but if you feel in your gut that this change is what is needed in order for you to be successful, then, personally, I would make it.

We will go into this in greater detail in Chapter 5 – Pull Out the Weeds That Keep Growing Back, but something that is affecting whatever quest you're on and causing failure could be the people close to you. This is an example of an internal factor for failure but one masked as an external factor. Yes, they are another person, and they may be the contributing factor to this failure, but it is you who has decided to keep them around or let them have that much of effect on the outcome of what you're trying to achieve. Sometimes these people can be your partners: for example, they don't like the idea of you doing bigger and better things and they hold you back because of their own self-esteem issues. This can be friends and colleagues too, and it's a stark reminder of how important it is to surround

GROW FROM FAILURE

yourself with positive supportive people. If you do not, then this is the kind of change you may have to make. People will have an effect on the outcome of your success, positively or negatively, based on whether they are a positive or negative influence in your life. I say this because it's not always obvious when you're in the friendship/relationship, so do not be surprised if sometimes the change you are faced with is a person. If this person is slowing you down by getting in the way or making you question everything, then maybe they aren't the most appropriate person to keep close to you or your goals as you go through this journey? And maybe some tough decisions will have to be made.

Another change that is not always obvious can be your environment, so the change you may need to make can be about the physical. The place where you stand may not allow for the growth you seek, so you may need to up sticks and look for more fertile ground. For example, when I am coming up with new video ideas, and even as I'm writing this book, I find I'm more creative and my ideas flow better when I'm in light open spaces (i.e. sometimes we can only think as far as the four walls around us). Maybe the country you live in does not have the opportunities you seek? So, the change you may need to make can be as simple as moving rooms or it could be as large as moving towns and counties. Change is important in life, and it will definitely aid you when it comes to analysing your failure. When you embrace change after failure, you are encouraging new opportunity and growth.

> It is now on you to take action, to take what you have learned, decide what needs to be adjusted or what needs to change, and go for it again, unblinking, unwavering, then go again. Remove the negative influences, such as unsupportive people, and bring in positive influences, as in creative environments. Find your creative muse, remove distracting hobbies. Whatever the change may be, if it gets you closer to the success you require, then do it. This is the most productive way to handle failures and will keep you on the straight and narrow.

Detach from results

If what you are trying to achieve requires results along the way or one final result at the end from your effort, then a superpower for your confidence and eventual accomplishment is to learn how to detach from results. Results are what most people will measure you on, yourself included. The boss who has set you targets, the housemate or partner who has very firm standards of cleanliness and holds you to them, the running partner who wants to do 10k on a Sunday . . . results are everywhere. And people may not give you a second glance if you don't provide a positive result, and maybe (wrongly) you won't be happy with yourself either until you provide a positive result. This can have a damaging effect on our self-esteem because when we put such

GROW FROM FAILURE

an importance on the result of each attempt, then any setback or failure can feel like a punch to the gut. Instead, I recommend you reframe each result as an attempt, one of many that will result in the ultimate end result: happiness and success.

Your first few attempts may not yield the results you want. Meeting someone you like and asking them out may not go the way you want, for example. You may be trying to grow a home business, but the initial sales you get may not be what you want or expect. These results and outcomes can really get us down. Sometimes our self-esteem takes a body blow and we question whether this is really what we should be doing. You might think: maybe I'm just not good enough? These thoughts are unhelpful and unwelcome, because if everyone who ever attempted something and it didn't go the way they wanted let these thoughts win, we would never have Apple, never have Harry Potter, never have Forrest Gump, never have Disney!

Detaching from results is not easy as we generally attach ourselves (or our sense of ourselves) to the results. Our ego gets attached because we are the one failing or succeeding, and we then go on to think that we are a failure or a success based on the result. This then hinders our experience of the task and potential overall success, but that shouldn't be the case; we are someone attempting to achieve something, and if that fails then we are just someone still in the process, not an actual failure. So we really need to detach the result from us and our ego. Whatever you are trying to accomplish is not *you*. You are not the failure, and you are not the result. This is the mindset you need to adopt. You are you: a person who has attempted to gain a date with a handsome stranger; you are not a dateless failure. You are attempting to start a business and learning what works and what doesn't; you are not a business failure.

LinkedIn marketing insider Dharmendra Kumar states in an article on LinkedIn: 'When we're attached to the outcome, our happiness is dependent on external factors that are beyond our control. We become trapped in a cycle of seeking pleasure and avoiding pain. Detachment, on the other hand, allows us to cultivate a sense of inner peace and happiness that is independent of external circumstances. It helps us to find joy in the process of doing, rather than in the outcome.'

You need to care less about the result and concentrate more on the journey. Your journey is constantly progressing, and it never stays still for long enough to form a label around you. As well as coming to terms with the fact that we will probably fail along the way, we have to accept that we do not know when we will succeed. Once we get there, and realise that success is not necessarily as fixed a point as we thought, it will help us to understand the importance of enjoying the journey and being analytical in our approach to the method. Hyperfocusing on the end of the journey will burn you out faster than anything.

I always wanted to meet my perfect partner, get married and have a family (especially as my own was so disjointed as I was growing up), and in pursuit of that I dated a few girls over the years. Most of my relationships did not go the way I wanted and did not go the way of my dream scenario, but I feel I have now, however, met my perfect partner. If I had hyperfocused on

GROW FROM FAILURE

that dream, then either I would have forced a past relationship to be something it wasn't (as none of those were really right for me, else they would have worked out), or I would have got so discouraged after each breakup because it didn't supply the results I wanted. I may well have avoided that pain altogether and given up. Instead, I detached and gave myself the air to think and re-evaluate. I didn't put a deadline on finding this girl. All I had to do was keep putting myself out there and be better than the last time.

This approach allows you to be focused and, in the end, actually achieve your goal in a more productive way. Being so concerned by the results will stress you the heck out, but detaching from it allows you to stay focused and present, enjoying the effort. Ideally you'll get to a point where you can approach the task at hand with a sense of peace and calm, enjoying the process in the knowledge that you are trying your best in this situation with what you have.

> To help you achieve all this, I recommend you write down in a journal what it is you're trying to achieve and ask yourself if you are focusing too much on the result rather than enjoying the process. Write down where you can change your focus (improvements over failures, for example) and what things you can do to enjoy the journey more. Looking back at the journey will help you to realise how far you've come as well, which is usually a good motivator.

Practising self-compassion

Modern life is highly pressure-oriented. Sometimes it can feel like a rat race, especially with all the comparing that happens in society, as so much of life seems like a competition: who has the best job, who has the best family and who has the prettiest home. Instead of just being proud of other people, we can sometimes feel jealous and a pressure to have it all figured out. We think we must be the best or we must work harder to keep up. This is crazy and unrealistic, and it has caused so many of us to be overly self-critical of ourselves and our failures. Telling ourselves we need to do something or be something to be a better person, when, in fact, we should be focusing on healing what makes us feel this way in order to find contentment.

A stress survey commissioned by the Mental Health Foundation has found that six out of ten young people, aged 18–24, have felt so stressed by the pressure to succeed they have felt unable to cope.

We don't allow ourselves to believe that we might actually just be good enough as we are. The article suggests this leads us to being overly self-critical, which can lead to mental health complications, and in some cases this is an incredibly hard trap to get out of. As we've discussed in other chapters, chasing this idea that we need more to be happier doesn't deliver happiness. Instead, we need to heal what it is inside us that makes us subscribe to this thought. This is where we need to practice self-compassion.

GROW FROM FAILURE

An article on self-compassion from Calm.com suggests: 'Some people think self-compassion is just about feeling good about yourself. But it's more than that. Self-esteem is often about how we compare to others – are we better, smarter, or more successful? And it isn't always the most productive measure of worth. Self-compassion isn't about comparing. It's about accepting yourself as you are, with all your strengths and weaknesses.'

Not to be confused with self-pity, self-compassion doesn't allow you to wallow in the negative but encourages you to reframe your thinking in a positive direction. As I explained earlier, being overly critical of ourselves will put us on a downward spiral, and this is a serious enemy to living a good life. Instead of looking at life like it's competition and being overly self-critical, we need to put an emphasis on self-care through self-compassion and there are a few ways you can do this:

- Start with mindfulness through meditation.
- Take yourself to a quiet place to sit or lie down (I often do this in the bath).
- Turn over these critical thoughts in your mind and simply notice the thoughts without being judgemental about them.

When we position a thought outside of us rather than as part of us, we see the thought for what it is, which most of the time is unfounded and unneeded. Practicing mindfulness before taking action on these critical thoughts will help you make the right decision, especially when handling failure.

Before I practiced mindfulness, I would find so many ways to cut myself down. I would tell myself that I wasn't smart enough to do certain things, not good-looking enough to keep a girlfriend, and not interesting enough to ever achieve anything. But giving myself the space to zoom out on these thoughts helped me to find they had no legs, that they were born from insecurity and based on absolutely no evidence, just useless and damaging comparisons to others. I always assumed everyone who was anyone had achieved something because they had something I didn't, but for the majority, this is not the case. If you plan, apply yourself, take action and never give up, you are capable of achieving anything.

One of the main benefits gained from mindfulness is awareness of our emotions and how much they can change or be affected by outside influences, and this is key for self-compassion. It helps you to be more aware when these thoughts are happening so that you can cut them down before they build up and weigh you down. It is also key to being aware of others. Realise your common humanity: you are not alone in this world and this challenge you face will have most definitely have been attempted by others before you. Think about how others would react when facing the same challenges. What you're going through, and your thoughts, are incredibly normal: you are not alone here, as we are all human, and the majority of us have to deal with these thoughts and challenges regularly.

This also opens us up to another self-compassion exercise:

GROW FROM FAILURE

treating yourself like your best friend. Think about what would happen if others, especially those close to us, were going through this situation, tackling this same challenge as we are now, and finding it as difficult as we are . . . What would you say to them? How would you motivate them and show them encouragement? Once you have your answer, say these exact things back to yourself. Offering yourself a positive inner monologue will go a long way to destroying negative thoughts that aren't helping you. This does need practice, but it's key for self-compassion and building confidence. A useful way that you can do this is to set up the issue or situation in your head or write it down, but change it from being your issue *you're* working through to one of your friends or family members might be facing. Then, what advice would you give *them* to help them get through it? Seeing the situation in this light, and taking a step back, will allow you to think a little more clearly about a solution.

Self-compassion is a core pillar in improving your overall satisfaction with life. When done properly, through the exercises I've shared above, it can help build mental and emotional wellbeing. It will help you to reduce stress and anxiety, leading you to feel happier and more content. It manifests a growth mindset as self-compassion can help you look at mistakes and failings in a new light, labelling them as new challenges to overcome, ones that will help you to learn and grow.

Life will throw many challenges your way, so being comfortable with that knowledge sets you up for success. Do not act shocked when they arise as you have the tools to handle them. This is not the first challenge you have faced, nor will it be the last, and maybe you have multiple goals you want to achieve. Self-compassion makes you better equipped in handling them, and you will be able to bounce back quickly after each one.

Looking at the bigger picture

> 'Let me fall if I must fall. The one I am becoming will catch me.'
>
> BAAL SHEM TOV

We've discussed a lot about how important failure is to your timeline and journey, but that's not to say it will be easy. More likely the opposite; it will be bloody hard, and each time you put yourself out there and fail, it's going to hit you like physical pain. I'm going through it right now as I write this chapter. Outside of writing, I'm in the process of adjusting my social media content (I'm always looking for ways to improve and social media is a rapidly changing game), but it's not going the way I expected. It's not really working out, so far. Because it's new, has different visuals, and is more than likely not expected by my audience, it hasn't performed well in a metrics sense. And I'm finding the fact that it's not meeting my expectations painful and a little hard to take. I don't say this to scare you or put you off, but because I don't want you to be shocked

GROW FROM FAILURE

when it happens to you and you have to feel what I'm feeling. I want you to be able to accept failure and not let it knock you off-balance. Because life doesn't wait for you, it doesn't feel sorry for you, it doesn't say 'oh, poor Alex – his content isn't working right now, so I'll throw him a bone.' No, I have to keep showing up, no matter how bothered about my failure I might feel. You've got to do this sh*t even when you're sad, heartbroken or tired. Life doesn't care and it waits for nobody. So, I have to learn, I have to plan; maybe make a change and then go again, even though there's a high chance it won't work out then either. How do I do it? How are you expected to keep going, time and again, regardless of fear, failure and pain?

The answer is by focusing on the big picture. Zooming out, to look at the current moment in the context of not just the whole project but also your grander plans across years or even your whole life, allows you to see everything in terms of one step along a bigger path. And this takes you out of any current funk. Not just how you feel right now, in the centre, but in the beginning, and the end.

> Let's start with the beginning: think about where you started from. What were your drivers and pain points? Remind yourself of them and write them down. How far have you come since then? Probably a lot further than you expected. Look back at what you did to get to this point, and if you have faced challenges and failures ... how did you handle those early failures? Looking at the

> bigger picture and remembering how far you've come, as well as the reasons you started in the first place, are fantastic motivation when you have to get back up after a knock down.

In addition to this, see the downs as just as vital as the ups and you will begin to enjoy the journey, enjoy the process. As we have discussed, if you can truly enjoy where you are, without having to succeed to make you happy, then you'll be better placed to actually find satisfaction in the end result. Zoom out and see it all. You're doing incredibly well: your past would be proud, and your future is bright. And there will always be some lows (that's a personal note to myself as well) but that's not the whole story.

This is all a test to see if you really want it

> 'I asked life, why are you so difficult? Life smiled, and said, "People don't appreciate easy things".'
>
> UNKNOWN

As the above quote rightly points out, with any goal, life is testing you to see if you actually want it and deserve it. It's true we don't appreciate the easy things. We are far more likely to

GROW FROM FAILURE

cherish and hold on to something we worked our socks off to get. If you really want it, you have to hurt for it.

Now I don't necessarily mean putting in tons of hours of gruelling work, but I mean the work that gets you out of your comfort zone, the work that scares you, the stuff that makes you second-guess everything, and the work that you keep at, regardless of failure. The presence of failure is essential to the achievement of any goal because you must have placed this mission high up in the clouds for a reason, either because it represents the zenith of what you hope to achieve or because it's so unlikely that it is referred to as something unreal . . . a dream. And if you succeeded too quickly or without any challenges, was it ever a dream for you in the first place?

At 19 years of age, Lady Gaga was signed by Def Jam Recordings and three months later, they let her go. They had got her in, heard her sing, started making a single and didn't like it, so they didn't see her as worth the time or money it would need to continue. She could have easily given up after that brutal rejection and heck, most people would. But she didn't: she was hungry, she took the failure, learned from it and went back to working at it. She was determined and understood the assignment. A year later, Interscope Records signed her up, and the rest is history.

Don't overreact or overcorrect (i.e stay calm under pressure)

We discussed previously what actions to take when faced with a setback or failure, the main thing being to learn and readjust before taking another swing. I want to flag, however, that this doesn't mean you should scrap everything and start again. The idea here is to build on what you know, adding blocks and building upwards instead of knocking everything down and starting again. Imagine your life and goals as a house: you've lived in this house for a while, but now it's not to your liking, so you want to change the shape and the way it looks, but the house has a good structure to it (as they say, it has good bones), so it would be a waste of energy and resources to demolish it. But what you can do is renovate it. Take what is good and what exists already and build around it. And that's how we should look at our tasks and goals. A setback doesn't mean we've failed *completely*, and so we shouldn't start from square one; we just take what we've learned so far and add to what we've already got, and if we need to remove something to test it, then we do so.

We need to make sure we don't overreact because this can lead to more failure, which could be completely unnecessary. It's tough to face failure, but just because something didn't go the way we wanted it to, that doesn't make us a failure, so we need to make sure we don't overcorrect and knock down what we did do well along the way. This can be devastating

GROW FROM FAILURE

to our progress, because we will often face failure (arguably more so than success), so if we knock the house down every time, then the house never gets built and your dream never becomes a reality.

In Bob Rotella's book on golf psychology, *Golf is Not a Game of Perfect*, he shares multiple examples of professional golfers who allowed poor results to eat away at their confidence and destroy their careers. Seve Ballesteros was a great example. His career was ended by just one poor shot at the Masters in 1986, as that one shot made him overthink everything, and rather than focusing on what he did do well, he only concentrated on the bad shot and this ate at his confidence until he had nothing left. If we are too scared to face failure and accept that it is part of the process, then we are much more likely to tear the house down in the belief that everything is wrong.

So, beyond accepting the presence of failure, how do we avoid overcorrecting and overreacting? One of the main ways is to remain as calm as possible when faced with adversities and challenges. When we are calm under pressure, we are less likely to make silly mistakes. Because in calmness (as opposed to stressed, worried and worked up), we can think more clearly, solutions come with clarity, and we don't jump to correct too quickly. So, the question here is how can you remain calm when faced with failure?

We discussed mindfulness earlier in this chapter and, of course, that is a tried-and-tested way of remaining calm in this sort of situation, but there's a few other ways we can look at it.

Susan Tardanico suggested in *Forbes* magazine, in an article about facing failure, that we should do our best not to take it personally:

'Separate the failure from your identity. Just because you haven't found a successful way of doing something (yet) doesn't mean you are a failure. Personalising failure can wreak havoc on our self-esteem and confidence.'

To be calm we must stop dwelling on failure and letting it get us down. You are not the only one who has failed. I have shown you several examples of successful people who have faced multiple failures and still managed to find a way to succeed (myself included). Failure did not stop them, and they did not let it consume them. It doesn't matter how much you think and worry about the failure as it won't change the outcome. You cannot change the past either, and you don't want to, as you need failure, you need to have a healthy relationship with it. You need to learn to become great, and failure is the ultimate teacher for that. You shouldn't wish the challenge not to exist, instead focus on how you can use it to shape your future.

5

PULL OUT THE WEEDS THAT KEEP GROWING BACK

Looking after ourselves is a lot like looking after a garden, and so I am going to use that metaphor quite freely in this chapter. While it may initially seem silly to compare the two, go with me and hopefully it will become a useful visualisation exercise that will help you look at yourself as being like a constantly changing ecosystem that, like a garden, needs maintenance to stop it reverting to its wild state, a state that we are arguably trying to tend and nurture to transform it into something beautiful.

So, without further ado . . . welcome to your garden. Right now, and certainly during bad patches in your life, I'm going to assume it needs some work. The lawn (your self-esteem) is not in great shape, and you've got a few tufts of grass here and there, while most of the grass is burned yellow from the sun, having not been watered in a while. This means there's no pretty flowers yet (your accomplishments). And then there are weeds. They are taking up space and stunt any other floral growth, and seem to come back over and over again. You'll need some sturdy gloves (strong mindset) for this job, as looking after your garden is a tough and consistent task, but an incredibly rewarding process. After all, it's *your* garden, and you want to make it as spectacular as it can be.

So far within this book, we have discussed many things you might be doing internally to hinder your own growth and what actions you should take to counter this and to build a better life for yourself. After all, this book is about how we get out of our own way, and it's great that we're here to recognise that. However, there may be something else holding you back, or should I say someone else holding you back. That's right: the weeds are other people.

The reason I have decided to include this in a book about how we hold ourselves back is because, while other people may be seen as more of an external than internal source for our unhappiness, I want to help you understand that it is actually through our own choices that these people remain in our lives. And if, in the case of family, we didn't get a choice, then it is still us who have decided every day to either keep them around or not set healthy boundaries with them. Even if at times it feels like other people are what is stopping you, really *you* are in control of everything that involves you becoming a happy and successful version of yourself. And it's important to recognise that, because once you do, you can start to pull out the weeds.

PULL OUT THE WEEDS THAT KEEP GROWING BACK

Forgiving people who have wronged you

There are many ways other people hold us back and many reasons for it. Sometimes others put us down, sometimes people make decisions that impact us negatively, in small and large ways, and sometimes the largest of ways can be that they cause us to experience trauma, either directly at their hands or indirectly in their care. We discussed how to use trauma and how to move past it previously, but we haven't yet discussed how to deal with those involved and how they may still be holding us back.

Despite the trauma I experienced as a child because of his aggressive nature, my dad is still in my life (just about). But sometimes you cannot fully remove someone, and I had to move on with my life and build something in spite of it and him. I had to find a way to get past the trauma. I had to choose between either cutting him out or keeping him in my life, but whichever I chose, I knew I needed to find a way that would not allow the memory of him to affect me going forward. Moving past the trauma but also moving forward in my life, but with him involved in it, is the path I took.

Of course, every traumatic experience is different, and every person involved is different, so there is by no means a right or wrong way to handle this (what worked for me is not going to work for everyone), but this is a way I personally found the most useful in ensuring the trauma and the person involved did not affect my present and my future. It's incredibly easy to allow our traumatic experiences to stop us going forward because they inevitably affect our self-esteem, and so any reminder of it, even years later, will bring up the trauma and make us feel like we are going backwards emotionally. So, you might find that the person in question doesn't even have to be with you physically, as just the memory of them can trigger you. This slows us down, fills our head with doubt and ultimately stops us from going out and achieving the life we want. So how do we stop this feeling of regression from happening and start to move forward?

Whatever trauma you're facing may have happened recently or be firmly in your past; it may have been caused by a bad breakup or from experiencing betrayal. It may have been physically or emotionally damaging (or both), but one thing that unites the majority of traumas is that the sufferer is often making a conscious choice to retain those emotions. If you are stuck in one place thinking about what happened to you, you are deciding to keep that event, and the people associated with it, with you. But we have to find a way to move past all this, and the most effective way I have found in stopping these nightmares from blocking us in the here and now is through forgiveness.

Abigail Brenner MD has stated, in *Psychology Today*: 'Forgiveness frees you. It allows you to take your power back. You are no longer chained to an entity that saps your energy and takes the life out of you. And freeing yourself may allow you to see this person/situation in a whole different light. Instead of focusing on all the negatives, forgiving may allow you to remember all of the positives that once were.'

PULL OUT THE WEEDS THAT KEEP GROWING BACK

Forgiveness also allows you to get out of a mindset of feeling like the victim as *you* are the one making the decision to forgive. Of course some things are completely out of our control, but always seeing ourselves as the victim is damaging for growth, as it removes your agency. You may not have had control before, but you *do* have control now, and by no longer seeing yourself as a victim, you are no longer letting the negative energy dictate your life. Through this, you can focus on becoming stronger, building up your integrity and your character to the point where you feel like you can navigate those people or situations again.

But, as this is such a huge emotional leap, it's worth remembering that you are unlikely to move forward without practical steps. Just sitting down with the same emotions you've always felt is unlikely to work.

So, a great place to start, as ever, is to write things down. You can either journal about it or just get your Notes app out and write it there. Writing about a time when you were betrayed or even inadvertently affected by something can help you process what happened and ultimately move on. The real key here, however, is in the way you write it. Writing this down with a focus on positive outcomes can make the difference in the process of the forgiveness.

Research has suggested that if you journal about the benefits you've received or experienced from the event rather than obsessing over how they wronged you and how bad it made you feel, it has a far greater success rate in actually moving on from the situation. So, if you can, try to focus on what you learned from all this. Like I said in a previous chapter, my childhood trauma and bad breakups have got me where I am now and without them, I likely would never have dived into this self-improvement journey and been given the opportunity to share with you today. It really is worth finding the silver lining in all of this for you, and I promise you there will be one.

And don't forget: this can be an ongoing process. If you experience hurt at the hands of others, continue to write. I would suggest you write in a gratitude journal, so that you can keep your mindset in a positive space and not a negative one. Positivity breeds space for growth, while negativity shuts everything down (more on this later).

You can then decide if you want to tell the person or people in question how they've wronged you or affected you. Getting it all out on the table may be the best way for you to move past it, but if you're in a situation where you can't, or you think it will make everything worse, then just writing it all down and seeing it outside of your mind will help you move past it all and stop it from holding you back.

It's important to state that you can forgive in order to help you move on, but you don't need to keep that person in your life. If, by forgiving them, you can totally move on and create something amazing in your life with them still around, without the memory

PULL OUT THE WEEDS THAT KEEP GROWING BACK

hindering you, then that's fantastic, but, if not, then it might be best to release them completely: forgive them and physically let go of them. Either way, the memory or the presence of them should no longer affect you in going for what you desire.

> So, I believe, at this point, that it's better to get any hurt feelings towards others who have wronged us out of our heads and onto paper. As I've said so many times before, the simple act of writing your feelings down will go a long way towards removing the weight of the emotion. Write their name and how they have wronged you, but then write as many positives as you can possibly think of regarding what may have come from the experience and also any potential ones. For example, being dumped by a long-term partner has led or could lead to you meeting the love of your life. Putting a positive spin on your trauma will help you to forgive and move on for good.

Why people are mirrors

If you've ever worked in customer service, you will more than likely have come across a disgruntled customer who may well seem angry and irate over what you believe to be a minor inconvenience or something that you don't believe should be worth getting so annoyed about. Nowadays we call this phenomenon

'The Karens' (which is more than a little unfair on people named Karen everywhere, as the only one I know is lovely and would never be like this). However, the example I'm using, of someone going ballistic at a customer service worker over the smallest of issues, is a very real thing. The reason this happens is most commonly for a few reasons: one, maybe they aren't all that mentally sound today; two, maybe they've had a history of disappointment with the organisation they are yelling at; or three (and the most common reason), they are projecting.

Tanya J. Peterson, of Choosing Therapy, explains projection in her article on choosing therapy as: 'Projection is a type of psychological defence mechanism. When people project, they place their negative emotions, beliefs, or traits on someone else. People project to protect themselves from uncomfortable inner conflict and anxiety, but the behaviour can interfere with various relationships and situations.'

The person (or 'Karen') yelling at the poor shop worker is at the exaggerated end of projecting, but you have probably experienced someone projecting at a lower level fairly recently (and perhaps more times than you realise). Maybe it's a boss that's too harsh, your parents yelling at you for what seemed like an insignificant action, or perhaps someone close to you putting you down. Yes, quite incredibly, these people are speaking to you in this manner because they are struggling internally with something themselves.

Projection is a direct reflection of how they feel about themselves. You may even have done this yourself. Like many people, I find myself projecting when I'm extremely tired, sometimes

PULL OUT THE WEEDS THAT KEEP GROWING BACK

snapping at my loved ones over the smallest of things, which aren't really their fault, but because I'm sleep deprived and feel terrible about myself in those moments and am often overly anxious, I take it out on them. (Don't worry: I do make efforts to turn around and apologise when I realise what I have done. I'm very lucky I have forgiving people in my life.)

In these moments, the projector is avoiding responsibility for their inner feelings or desires by projecting how they feel (including, importantly, their level of self-esteem in a certain situation) onto another, external person. An example that is seen commonly in relationships is one person projecting issues onto the other partner, complaining about how messy their partner is, say, likely because they are concerned about being messy themselves.

Projection may be holding you back in a few ways. Firstly, it is possible you are the one projecting or, secondly, someone close to you could be projecting onto you and, as a consequence, holding you back. If you are the one projecting, you could be pushing away the people who matter most to you. Thankfully, though, there's a few ways to handle this.

The first method to avoid becoming the projector is to build your self-esteem. Building your self-esteem will allow you to understand your emotions better and learn either to change or accept them. Either way, becoming more comfortable with your personal thoughts and who you are is important. And another way to help you stop or slow down projection is to focus on mindfulness. Mindfulness is awareness of your internal emotional state and your surroundings: it focuses you on living in the present moment. Mindfulness will allow you to build awareness of your behaviour, hopefully catching you in the act before you do or say anything you regret. This awareness could help you understand your triggers and then help you to work on them and lessen their power, and lastly, slows down your reaction to everything. One of the core tenets of mindfulness is not reacting instantly to any situation that inspires an emotional reaction in you. Mindfulness teaches that whenever you experience anything, or anyone says anything to you, while it may feel instinctual to respond straightaway, resist the temptation and know you do not need to react in the moment. Give yourself five seconds and then come back. Allow yourself the space to contemplate what is happening and to find the correct reaction to it.

As for others in your life that you believe to be projecting onto you, you'll have to handle them with some skill. Firstly, your awareness of what they are doing is key – once you've identified what someone else is doing to you, make sure not to react back to them as this will only escalate the matter. Instead, show some sympathy and open up a conversation where they feel safe to talk to you about what the issue is. You can say something like: 'What are you struggling with? I see you're upset about this, but there seems to be more to it. Get it off your chest.' Hopefully this will work and maybe you can even help them avoid projecting in the future. The aim is to become a safe space for them, and the relationship can build from there.

To use an example, think of the age-old scenario of the wife yelling at her husband for watching sports on TV when he is supposed to be taking out the garbage. Yes, she's mad at him for not doing the task he said he would, but there's also a long list of other tasks he said he would complete but never did. While it may seem in the moment like it's just about the garbage, he is actually breaking promises on a regular basis and this has become a pattern of behaviour. This means she regularly feels unloved and unsupported, which causes her self-esteem to take a hit, as she just wants, through his actions, to feel that love. All of this has led her to now yelling at him about the garbage and he's perplexed as this particular task just doesn't seem like a big deal. People are mirrors and they will show you how they feel about themselves through the way they converse with you and treat you, so listen to what they are projecting and try to understand it, as this will help resolve the conflict.

How to stop convincing people of your worth

> 'A person's worth is measured by the worth of what they value.'
>
> MARCUS AURELIUS

You may have a dominant figure in your life, you may have made or are currently making life decisions because of that person. This is not limited to but could be a parent, mentor or partner. You make key decisions that will have a long-term effect on your life because you want their approval; you want them to think you're doing a great job, you require a pat on the back, and you are constantly trying to prove your worth to these people. Whether this person is domineering or not, they are a dominant figure in your life. Sometimes these people are controlling and will actively limit your decision-making, or you may have put this person on a pedestal and they may have never chosen this particular role in your life, and, ultimately, you are making key life decisions to impress them just because you like them. Either way, this is not healthy for you *or* them. You now need to focus your life on making the big life decisions based on what you want for you, and not because you're seeking approval from someone else.

This idea of convincing others of our worth probably started back in school. We want to make friends and most of us initially want to do well academically. We feel the need to prove our worth in the playground so that we are not left out of games and friendships, and we want to prove we are good enough academically to our teachers and parents, so we get praise and approval, and hopefully do well in our education. In school this may have worked, but here's why it is counterintuitive in everyday life.

According to an article by Tom Ferry, CEO of Your Coach, the need for approval has been conditioned within us since birth: 'Approval from others gives us a higher sense of self-esteem. We're convinced that their recognition matters to our self-worth and how deeply we value ourselves.'

Let's start with friendships and relationships. I want you to hear me when I say you are *you* – you have a personality, a set of

PULL OUT THE WEEDS THAT KEEP GROWING BACK

skills and a conscience. When you try to expand or exaggerate any of these so that someone likes you, they aren't meeting the *real* you. They are meeting a version of you that won't always exist and, in turn, this will eventually push people away when the mask drops because you are no longer what they expected. And when you go on to make life decisions, like picking a job or a partner, and you have selected these based on whether you think someone else will see you as worthy because of your decision, you are not fully making that decision yourself, based completely on what you want. You won't enjoy your choice because it wasn't made for you, it was made for someone else. You will find no satisfaction because of this and it is highly likely, after you get the approval or the thumbs-up from this person on the pedestal, they will forget what you've done and go about their lives, while you've made a massive decision that will continue to affect your life for a long period of time.

If you believe you have to convince another person of your worth because you think they don't already know it, then you are already accepting less than you are worth. You are continuously putting yourself in the mould of a salesperson, selling yourself, and if you have to keep convincing people of your worth, it will be exhausting. When you go to a used car lot, the salesperson will try to convince you to buy a car because they think this is the right car for you. They will tell you about this or that feature because they have to convince you to make the purchase. A high-end car dealer like Ferrari will welcome you into the store and thank you for coming, but they will never have to sell you on the car because the car speaks for and sells itself. That's right: you're the Ferrari. Up to this point in your life you have spent too much energy trying to convince people of your worth instead of letting yourself and what you represent – your authenticity – do the talking. I don't care if it's a love interest or your parents or a boss. If you have to show off, if you have to exaggerate, and if you have to sell the idea of you to them, they do not belong in your life. You are enough just as you are, so start removing these people from the equation and make moves based on what *you* want.

A reminder for when you find yourself in these situations: you did not wake up today to convince other people of your worth. If there is someone in your life that you feel you need to constantly prove your worthiness to, continuing to do so will not make them magically realise or understand your worth if they haven't already. The right people for you will never put you in a position where you have to question your own worth. Just you, as you are, is enough. So let me ask you a question: if we no longer need to convince the people we know of our worth, do we need to convince those we don't know?

I ask this question because so many of us do try to convince complete strangers of our worth. We sometimes do this on social media or sometimes just by the way we are in public and with our appearance. We have no relationship with these people but think, for some reason, they should care about us. We need to let go of people who pay us no attention. We need to stop trying to make them care about us and our life and not get frustrated or angry when they take no notice. As you've probably realised throughout this book, this is mostly

PULL OUT THE WEEDS THAT KEEP GROWING BACK

a solo journey. We do not need to bring people on this ride with us. Let them have their own journeys and we will concentrate on ours. If you want people to care about your rise or transformational journey, well, you're probably doing this for the wrong reasons to start with. When you complete your goals and reach your dreams, the people who truly matter to your life will be there at the end, but they don't need to be there for the journey. This journey is for you and no one else.

You can't force anyone to care about you. You can't force them to be the person you need them to be. You can, however, choose to have people around you that support you. Really take a minute to pause to think and question if the path you're taking is actually for you. Because if you try to accomplish anything merely to gain the attention of someone who doesn't currently care about you, then it is highly likely they won't care regardless of your achievements, and, even worse, if they do magically turn around and say 'Oh, now I see you', then they are doing it for the wrong reasons, and what you have together would have been built on superficial greed and inauthenticity.

But it's my mission to help you realise that your self-esteem doesn't depend on the approval of others. You must forge your own path and move through this adventure regardless of if your parents, friends or even your partner approve. It's incredibly easy to be swayed by these people because, of course, they are important people to you, but if you believe what you're doing is the correct decision, then you have to follow your gut and your intuition. There are a few great ways to do this: when you get the urge to seek out approval, ask yourself why you think you need this approval. Is it because you're in a vulnerable state? Don't search for approval; instead search for why you think you need approval and work on the cause of that. Most of the time you'll realise that you really do not need it. Instead, sit with your feelings of fear and neediness. Learn to be comfortable with these feelings and push on regardless.

Your next step is to bring someone into your life who is completely objective. Unfortunately, most people are selfish (yes, including your parents) and will try to change the course of your decision-making based on what's best for them. So, instead, find that person who has no investment in your decision either way. These people can be trusted to give you objective feedback and, as long as they have relative experience in the subject, then they can be incredibly useful.

> When it comes to you making life decisions – for example, changing career or even following a new way of life – you will find it incredibly beneficial to write it all down and then, in a spider diagram, write down all the reasons why you are making this decision. Be completely honest with yourself, as some of the reasons will be based on what you want for yourself, but some might be related to wanting approval or trying to impress someone else, or even fear of missing out. If there are more reasons based on trying to convince someone else of your worth or because you want someone else to care about you, then this is not the right path for you.

PULL OUT THE WEEDS THAT KEEP GROWING BACK

How they have no accountability

It's dangerous for your overall success and happiness to believe everyone has your best interests at heart, as most people will try to influence your decision-making based on their own needs. This sounds more sinister than it is, but it's actually very common. To be completely selfless in everything you say would be a rarity. Of course we want what's best for other people, as we're not evil and do not wish for anyone's downfall, but if a decision they have to make has a negative effect on us, then we are more than likely going to say something to help swing that decision in our favour. For example, let's say you are offered a fantastic new job, but it will involve late hours or is far away and involves either a big commute or less time at home. Your partner might not want you to take the job as they don't want the relationship to become strained or end, so they may advise you not to take it. This could arguably be seen as for the benefit of the relationship, which you share, but ultimately you then have to live with that decision and will lose out on something, while they will not. This is an example of how, really, they have no accountability for your decision, as their life continues unaffected.

If you're low on self-esteem as it is, then you'll be likely to agree with their needs over your own. You may have a happy relationship, as a result of your joint decision, but you will have missed out on what could have been a life-changing opportunity. Every day you might be thinking: what if I made that jump? Every day you might have to face a job you hate; feeling depressed constantly because you didn't seek a change that was made for you. You have to live with your life choices, others do not. You are accountable for all these decisions while others are not.

When you go through your life and put other people's opinions above your own, you end up living your life on their terms, not yours. You might end up regretting these moments because you didn't live a life truly authentic to who you are. That person and whatever the opinion was that swayed your decision-making may no longer be around, and you're left with the outcome.

People are also human and therefore fallible, so, inherently, they will change their mind from time to time, and it can be devastating if you make a decision based on their thoughts and feelings, only for them to change their mind later on. And they can be a lot more flippant as it isn't their life they're dealing with. I used to work with someone who left their job because their partner didn't like them doing it. For the sake of the relationship, they quit and went into a line of work that they weren't necessarily excited about but that was approved by their partner. Three months later, they broke up. Multiple reasons were to blame for the breakup, but if they had made the decision based on what they thought was best for them and not their partner, at least they would still have had the role they loved, whatever happened in the relationship. You might be thinking it's the easiest option to go with another's opinion, because then you can say 'well, it wasn't my choice', if

PULL OUT THE WEEDS THAT KEEP GROWING BACK

it doesn't work out, but you yourself still have to live with the consequences. Only you know what makes the most sense for you. You should really trust your own intuition. Deep down, you know what's right for you, but you just might be a little scared of making the leap or speaking up. Don't worry: we can all be like this, so you aren't alone in this thinking, but if you really want to turn your life around, you must grab the reins, be the decision-maker, and own the result.

Then, when you succeed, you can be proud of yourself and it'll hopefully build your self-esteem, because you made the tough choices that got you to a point of success. And if you make some mistakes along the way, then you can work to fix them, because you know you are in charge. Don't relinquish control to someone else who can wipe their hands of you the moment it gets hard or it doesn't work out. This is what I mean about accountability . . . the more you own it, the more you're able not only to enjoy the positives, but know you have the power to turn around the negatives. If you make a mistake, make it on your own terms.

Pulling out the weeds

So, who are these people, the weeds? To be honest, they can be anyone: your best friends, your partner, your colleagues, your boss or quite often your parents. Anyone that you have allowed to have a say in how you run your life and anyone who tries to dictate how you think or feel. Your job now is to recognise these people for who they are and remove them from your garden. You need to pull them out so that what you want to grow can grow. Remember, though, pulling them out and removing them from your garden doesn't necessarily mean removing them from your life completely. We have other options we can take before reaching that point.

> So, look at your life as it is now. Get that pen and paper out and think about who it is that you're letting hold you back. Who is stopping you from moving forward with the life you deserve? And then we must take action. Write down why you believe they are holding you back. Are they being controlling? Or do they have your best interests at heart? Now decide if you need to discuss some boundaries with them or cut them out of your life completely.

While it's a great start to work on our self-esteem, choose ourselves over others for once, and trust in our own intuition, this doesn't stop other people from trying to change your mind or even trying to control you. As long as these people are close, there's always a chance they will try to influence your life and decision-making, and then there's always a chance that you will let them.

When it comes to addiction, counsellors will teach addicts

PULL OUT THE WEEDS THAT KEEP GROWING BACK

not to avoid their vices by doing something opposite or avoiding any chance of being tempted. The reason for this is that avoidance doesn't fix the root cause of the addiction and leaves you susceptible to relapse. The counsellors find it's more effective if the addicts can work on the root cause of the addiction and overcome it by facing it, so we will do the same for these intrusive compadres of yours. Besides, these people could be someone very close to you and you can't completely cut them out of your life (yet), because, firstly, you may not want to and, secondly, that might be incredibly difficult and not worth the headache. So, the first step in trying to stop these people influencing you is to set some boundaries.

Boundaries are a path for others to follow in regards to how they interact with you; you will tell them things you like or are okay with, and also state things you do not like and will not put up with. For example, if you are not okay with physical touch, setting out some boundaries with this person is a great and healthy way to avoid that from happening without the relationship completely breaking down.

Melissa Urban from Thrive Global puts it this way in her article on why setting boundaries is important: 'Boundaries allow those who care about us to support us in the way we want to be supported. They provide a clear line between what we find helpful and harmful, so people don't have to try to read our minds.'

We want to introduce boundaries in a healthy way. What we don't want is for you to get triggered by this person's controlling behaviour and then react in a negative way, potentially screaming at them about how much you hate their action or behaviour. For example, if your parents tell you how you should live your life but you're already a grown adult who is living it. Acting this way towards them will not work; it will get their back up, they will become defensive, and it's highly likely they won't hear the message you're trying to convey, leading to them potentially doing it again down the line. They think they have your best interests at heart, even if what they are saying is unhelpful to you. What is best practice is to bring this boundary up with them, either when they are calm or just after they have shown you an example of this behaviour, and then calmly explain to them that you don't appreciate it, explain how you don't need their opinion as you haven't asked for it, that you still appreciate them as a person, but in this case *this* action they are taking has *this* effect on you and how it makes you feel.

Not every single person will react well to this, because nobody likes to hear how they are having a negative effect on another person, but hopefully they will be self-aware enough to realise this is better for your relationship if they stop. Setting boundaries protects your happiness and your future, and these boundaries can be with friends, family members and/or partners – it allows you to flourish in whatever your mission is without being held back, or being tempted to let someone hold you back, and it also gives them the chance to keep their relationship with you but in a healthier environment. Some people will think what they are doing by telling you to live a certain way, or trying to convince you of a different path, is

PULL OUT THE WEEDS THAT KEEP GROWING BACK

doing right by you. However, for one simple reason, they are *not* doing right by you: it isn't *your* choice based on what *you* want. What they are suggesting may well be a good choice, but it may not be right for you. Only you can decide that.

Sometimes, however, someone just can't accept your boundaries. They either flat out reject them or they accept them in the moment but then repeat the unwanted behaviour. For example, your friend keeps meddling in your relationship. They don't like your partner, so they will take any chance they get to say something about them. You ask them to stop, but then a few weeks go by and they say something negative about them again. These people do not have a place in your life and, by keeping them close to you, you are only holding yourself back, because it is more than likely they will continue to bother you, continue to sway you and continue to stunt your progress.

This is why having boundaries is an important first step, because you are then in charge of sticking to your boundaries. In setting them, you are telling the other person this is something you don't like, and it has a certain effect on you. You are communicating clearly to them that you want to continue this relationship, but you expect your boundary to be respected. If it isn't, then you cannot continue the relationship (or any discussion on the topic), because they're showing that they do not respect you by not respecting your boundaries.

How you choose to deal with them not responding well is up to you: you can tell them that they have crossed your boundary, and you now need space from them, or you can just distance yourself straightaway because they were already warned. You need to remove anyone from your life who tries to control you and then doesn't respect your wishes that they stop. This is what self-love looks like, and it's imperative if you are to grow and become the person you want to be.

How to let go of people from your past

We have already discussed at length, in Chapter 2 – Engage With Your Past Trauma, how people from our past can affect us, but there is also another way in which we let them dictate our current actions.

You may be looking to create a life for yourself that someone from your past would have approved of. This can look like a past partner telling you they wished you had applied yourself at this or that, before going on to end the relationship, leading to you then thinking that they were right, or that you could win them back if you did apply yourself in whatever the idea was. But you don't want to make life plans for the wrong decisions. It doesn't matter if that person was right, as you're not looking to make a change based on something someone else wanted from your life. Making big life changes based on someone else's ideals will leave you feeling hollow and incomplete.

You need to let go of these people. They are no longer in your life and there's a reason for that. Thinking about them and what they would like for you is not of a growth mindset;

PULL OUT THE WEEDS THAT KEEP GROWING BACK

instead, it is built of insecurity in thinking that you, just as you are, are not enough. Building a life for you that you're proud of is the fastest way to be content.

Cassie from Upcycled Adulting has this to say: 'Unfortunately, much of the information our brains store that's meant to help us survive and even thrive is overgeneralised. And it may actually prevent us from moving forward and finding happiness ... Your past experiences and how you processed them affect every decision you make.'

> Letting go of these people is all about awareness. I want you to ask yourself: 'Why do you still care about what this person used to think?' If any answers come to you, then write them down. This is a brilliant first step. Then write down any thought patterns or pain that might be affecting you still. For example, thinking that even though these individuals are no longer in your life, they know you better than you know yourself and they would have known best. If you can recognise these unhelpful thinking patterns, having an awareness of them will help you to cut them dead when they pop into your head going forward. Underneath all this write down what is it that is still affecting your actions now and how this is holding you back. Why are you continuing to live for someone else? Actively seek that pain in your past, because there's a high chance that you aren't completely over it. Journal all of this and ask yourself this important

> question: what do you need to do in order to move past this and stop it from affecting your new chapter? Hopefully, by this point, you have an answer re: what you need to do, and then you need to make a promise to yourself that all future life plans are coming from *you* and not what *they* would have liked.

Take these steps and let go of the past and these people, because you deserve to live a new life designed by you and focused on what you believe to be the right steps for your happiness. You deserve to be unburdened of the past, and only when you achieve this can you explore, grow and live a fulfilling life.

Why you shouldn't tell people your goals

There isn't a problem with telling people very close to you, like your partner, what your hopes and dreams are. However, we shouldn't be shouting them from the rooftops and telling everyone about your plans. And there's a few reasons for this.

When you go about telling your friends or family your plans for your future, there's a very real chance that they will think about how your plans will affect them and, as discussed, this can have a negative impact. They may be your loving family, but most people will naturally and maybe subconsciously think about the affect this will have on them. Then it depends on who that

PULL OUT THE WEEDS THAT KEEP GROWING BACK

person is, but they may try to convince you it's not the best idea, or they might even try to guilt you into making another choice.

As I have said, you may want to ask the opinions of people very close to you, but you need to be aware that their reaction might not be what you expect and so you need to stay strong and not let it affect your decision-making.

The other reason why it is beneficial to keep your plans to yourself is something I never realised I was doing until I read about it. When we tell others about our plans, there is often a greater chance that we will not go on to fulfil those plans. The reason for this is because, when we talk about our goals and dreams to others, it feels good. We gain small hits of dopamine just talking about our exciting plans, so doing so actually ends up weakening the urge to actually go on to accomplish the dream, because we already feel good about it without having done the work.

When I first heard this, I was stumped, because I genuinely thought it would be the opposite. When I was younger and I cared a lot more what people thought of me, I would think that, if I told someone I was going to do something, I would then need to get it done because now they knew about it and, if I didn't do it, then in their eyes I might look like a failure. But when I looked back at all the plans and goals I had when I was younger and saw that most of them never came to fruition, I realised how real this phenomenon was. I always felt good when I'd meet up with friends and share my big plans with them; I would come away feeling great from the interaction, and this definitely slowed down my inspiration. When you add this to the fact that now I had also attached some level of responsibility to the idea because I had shared it, I suddenly became disengaged with the idea.

I genuinely believe it is better to keep things to yourself until they are already rolling and you've seen some level of success. The only person who knew I was trying to create a social media account to help others was my partner. This allowed me the space to make mistakes, experiment and enjoy it. It was my thing, and there were no judges and no pressure, and it flourished because of that.

I'm sure by now you've understood the message of this chapter, but here it is one last time: other people, regardless of your relationship with them, have no right telling you what you should do with your life and your plans. You need to make your own decisions, you need to make your own mistakes, and you need to live your timeline and journey. You do not need anyone's unasked opinion about what you're doing to achieve the life you want.

Your garden

Over time, you'll have a beautiful 'garden' to look at. You'll have either removed the weeds from your garden or transformed them into something useful, and the whole thing will look beautiful, thanks to the incredible achievements you have accomplished throughout your life. Look out for weeds and tend to the garden regularly, because that's what a happy life will require: regular upkeep and no interference from anyone else, so remove what you need to remove and enjoy the process.

6
BECOME ACCOUNTABLE

Understanding accountability

> 'It is easy to dodge our responsibilities, but we cannot dodge the consequences of dodging our responsibilities.'
>
> JOSIAH STAMP

Many people are working 50 hours a week in a job that they only do so they can afford rent and food. This all-too-familiar scenario can cause us to have no social life because of our work, and often we have no partner because there's just not enough time or we don't have the energy to show the love required to maintain a relationship, and each month there's something new we need to pay for that costs £10.99 a month. It is easy to get stuck in this trap, and unfortunately this is what a lot of people's lives look like. All the while most of us think that something will miraculously change and whisk us away from the monotonous cycle. But nothing changes without action and life doesn't change just because we wish it would. In fact, nothing good long term will happen to you until you understand this one simple concept: you are in charge of your own life; no one is coming to save you, no one is coming to make it better for you, and no one is going to give you a free ride to your ideal life.

This idea might feel like a bit of a slap in the face, but if it does feel that way, then good! It's time we woke up and realised this truth about life. And the faster we do this, the better for us and our future. We are raised, through no fault of our parents, to believe that something will just work out without much effort from us. For many of us, just the caring nature of our parents that ensured they kept us healthy and happy meant we received food, clothing, shelter and entertainment for the most part with no effort from ourselves. It's a basic requirement as we grow up, but it doesn't teach us how to do these things for ourselves when the time is right.

For many people, our families provide for us from birth until we are 18 or so. In some cases, our families will provide for us past that, going into our twenties and thirties, and while this may seem like a great safety net and give great comfort to those who need it, I'm not sure it's a good idea to rely so much on others. If we are looked after and not expected to fend for ourselves from the start of our adult life onwards, we

BECOME ACCOUNTABLE

will defer to others at the slightest sign of issues in our own lives. You most likely won't know how to work for something you want, you won't be able to handle the emotions and struggles that come with trying to achieve something on your own, and more than likely you will not even try, because you believe something will just happen and it will all somehow be okay, because that is what your history has led you to expect. This is believed by so many, but is actually a reality for very few people so we need to change to a mindset to acknowledge that only we can get ourselves to the place of our dreams – we need to be accountable for our own lives. We are accountable for everything that happens and everything we wish for from this point on. No one is to blame for our past nor our future, only we are.

Learning to trust yourself

Part of our journey to becoming accountable is learning to trust the person you put all your hopes and dreams in the hands of: you. To be confident that you can accomplish something incredible, then you have to trust in yourself to do it, to get you through it and not give up in the hard moments. This is where we need to start. Most people won't attempt anything because they don't trust themselves to complete whatever it is or stick with it, and this comes about for many reasons. Maybe they don't have the evidence to show they can or maybe they've tried things in the past but failed and so given up before they've had a chance to succeed. So how do we trust ourselves in these situations, and learn to trust ourselves going forward?

Benjamin Hardy, PhD, states in his LinkedIn article: 'Sadly, most people are living a lie. They don't keep commitments even to themselves. They don't accomplish their goals and dreams. They are bound by fears and other emotions they so desperately want to avoid. Nevertheless, if you're willing to do the hard interior work of living a life of trust and emotional freedom, there are absolutely no limits to your growth and potential.'

Here lies the first obstacle to learning to trust ourselves: commitments and promises. You may not believe you can do it because the last time you said you were going to get yourself in shape and start jogging, you gave up after one week. If you have a history of breaking promises to yourself, then it's totally fair that it will be hard to trust yourself again. But one way we can interrupt this pattern is to start small. Make much smaller commitments to yourself that will have an impact on your overall goal but will be much, much easier to achieve. For example, if your goal is to write a book, don't go head-on and try to write the book if you don't trust yourself to complete it. Maybe you've tried writing whole books before and it just hasn't worked, which is fair, as a book is a big undertaking. So, instead, write essays or short stories to get yourself used to the idea of writing, as this helps with creativity and confidence. Each time you complete a smaller project, you'll feel better about yourself and your chances to write this book, and it will boost your creativity as you'll have more confidence in your

BECOME ACCOUNTABLE

ideas. Complete as many small commitments as you can until you believe you can trust yourself to make a grander commitment. The smaller steps for our book idea can look like this:

> Plan plot ideas | Develop your characters | Plan for a purpose (what you want the reader to take away) | Pick a point of view | Write a sample introduction and chapter | Plan your writing schedule.
>
> All of these things are integral to writing a novel, but none have to be done all at once. As I've said, a book is big undertaking, and so is attempting anything you've never done before. It can be taxing on us mentally and physically, so to ease the anxiety of the task, learn to trust yourself, and you can do this by breaking the task down into manageable commitments.

> 'Happiness is when what you think, what you say, and what you do are in harmony.'
>
> MAHATMA GANDHI

All promises and commitments follow this rationale, including the day-to-day promises we make to ourselves, the ones we make on a regular basis. If you say you're going to do something, then do it. If you say you're waking up early tomorrow, then do it. If you say you're going to call your mum, then do it. You will start to love and trust yourself a lot better when you become a person of your word. Never underestimate the psychological damage we do to ourselves when we break these small promises, or the psychological benefits we can gain from, instead, keeping these small promises.

To be accountable is to take action in regards to your life; it's about going for what you want instead of waiting for it to happen. The longer you sit and do nothing, the longer you are in this perpetual state of limbo, where you don't know if you can or can't – you're just hopeful it will happen some other way, and then you will start to believe there's a strong chance you can't do it, or it won't happen, because it hasn't happened yet. But you will never truly know until you attempt it. The action of doing creates confidence that you can. You are doing, meaning you trust yourself.

Having trust in the process

Trusting the process will go a long way towards helping you become more accountable to yourself. A lot of people will shy away from going for what they want because it doesn't happen instantly, or the idea of something taking a year or two just makes them feel the thing is maybe not worth it. This is a comfort mindset and it's lazy. You are putting your future self at a disadvantage because you don't want to do the hard work now.

BECOME ACCOUNTABLE

By choosing the easy option and not putting in the work now, you are making your life easy today, sure, but it will only be harder later. It is far more important to choose discomfort now for an easier life later. For example, studying to gain a qualification that's needed for a career you'd like – the idea of studying alongside all the other stuff you've got going on seems like an exhausting task, and many people will think it's too much, so they won't take on the studying, instead continuing in the job they have. But then they wonder every now and then if they could have had a better career somewhere else. If we do the hard work, such as finding the space and time to study while working, then at least all that hard work and the stressful days will mean you set yourself up for better success in the future, instead of being in the same place and the same job still wondering. The easy option is only easy on you in the moment, but it has a reverberating negative effect on you in the long run.

In a *Washington Post* article on the growing change of children's ideal careers, when asked, almost 30% of children aged eight to 12 said they wanted to become YouTubers, per a survey from The Harris Poll. This is a huge percentage, and it only gets larger the older they get. Half of teenagers aged 13 to 18 dream of becoming a social media influencer, Morning Consult reports. Whether we need half of a generation being influencers is beside the point, but the sad thing about this is it won't become a reality for the majority of them. And this is not because of access or upbringing. All you need to become an influencer is a camera, a Wi-Fi connection, persistence and patience. And it's in those last two that our problem lies. The majority will not achieve this because they are not persistent or patient. Most won't even attempt it for fear that it won't work, and then those who do attempt it will drop it the moment it doesn't work. But I will tell you for a fact it *never* works the first time.

I'm someone who changes their online content quite a lot. The message is mostly the same, but how I package it will look different month to month. The reason for this is because I like to keep my following on their toes. I don't want to become stale and, also, not everyone learns the same way. Some people learn well from being told something by a face looking into a camera, some by reading short quotes, and some just need to be told it multiple times for it to sink in. And so, in my desire to inspire change in people, I mix it up. However, the perils of doing this is that not everyone will like the new style, or that it takes some people time to come around, and it's highly likely that my social media metrics will dip when I change. I'm okay with this, because, ultimately, I trust the process. I've done this enough times to see what works and what doesn't, and I believe in what I make, so I will keep putting it out there and not look to pivot every time a video doesn't do well.

And I trust the process because it has, over time, worked. Sometimes you have to trust in yourself, believe in what you're doing, and then just keep doing it until you see positive results. Of course there will be a limit for everyone; if you're failing for years, then maybe you need to change something up, but you need to be confident in the unknown and keep putting yourself out there, otherwise you may, for example, keep what you're doing the same way and suffer from people becoming bored, not engaging as much, or believing that you are out of touch with their current interests.

It took Mr Beast four years to get his first 1,000 YouTube subscribers. He posted relentlessly with barely any traction or notice. He trusted his process, though. He may have felt sh*t about himself and the platform, but he didn't let himself talk himself out of it. I do not believe that even 2% of the 13- to 18-year-olds who want to be social media influencers have the patience to do it for four years with no results. But what is four years? You have to experience those four years regardless, as time stops for no one, and four years will go surprisingly quickly, so why not spend the four years doing something that you believe in? Trust the process and come out the other side with something life-changing. Find a process you are happy with and then put your trust in it. If Mr Beast had not trusted in what he was doing, he wouldn't have amassed the 300 million subscribers he has, and YouTube would not be what it is today.

Getting an accountability buddy

Sometimes we all need a little help. I know it may come as a shock that that is coming from me, given that the majority of what we've discussed here focuses on how you should remain mostly alone in order to achieve your dreams and ambitions, and that, while your goals may involve other people, most of the time you're doing this alone. And it's good to accept that this journey of yours can be lonely, as even if you tell your partner or best friend about what you're doing, unless they are directly involved, they probably won't understand exactly what you're going through, so won't be able to connect. This is okay, because we should be accountable for our lives and not expect others to do it for us or even help us that much. But there is a certain person out there that can be incredibly helpful in regards to your success and who I will always say should be along for the ride, and that is the accountability buddy.

You're only just starting to learn how to become accountable, how to trust yourself, how to fall back on yourself and continue this mission without giving up. But having someone else who knows your aspirations, knows what it means to you, knows what your timeline and game plan is, will be of great help, because then they will be able to help you stay accountable.

So how do you choose your accountability buddy? Well, you can't just choose anyone, because they have to care enough about you and what you're doing. As I have mentioned in other chapters, people are naturally selfish, so you don't want to pick someone who potentially gains or loses from the results of your ambitions. If the person loses from your gain, then for obvious reasons they won't be the best person to cheer you on, because they just won't want you to achieve your goal. If someone gains a great deal from your success, this is also a no go, because the pressure of failing or letting them down would be too intense for this mindset we are building. Remember all of this is for

BECOME ACCOUNTABLE

you, not them, so don't give yourself the added and unnecessary pressure of disappointing them if you fail.

In the past I have chosen people who are going through the same thing as me, someone who has the same aspiration as me. When I was in my late teens, I was incredibly shy when it came to interacting with strangers, especially around girls I found attractive. One of my close friends had this same issue. We both wanted to be socially confident and to be able to talk to strangers with ease (and girls we liked). So, we agreed to be each other's accountability buddies, pushing each other outside of our comfort zones. We'd promise each other we weren't allowed to buy a drink in the pub unless we both spoke to strangers about something engaging. We'd also phone each other up to check in to see how we were doing. We'd set each other tasks that we both knew would help towards the overall goal. When you're not used to being accountable for yourself, having an accountability buddy can be a driving force that will help you reach your goals in a different way than if you were just on your own.

Suzy Reading, author and psychologist, believes that accountability buddies fall into two distinct categories: 'The first works more like a mentor where one person benefits from the other's wisdom; the second is when two people are focusing on a common goal. They can both work equally well.'

Reading puts this down to the rise of ritualised intimacy, something that has been in short supply in recent years.

'There's a huge element here around social connection and shared experience. Having a buddy you check in with at regular times to share your progress can make such a difference, not just to your goals but to your wellbeing.'

Having this person who helps you towards your goals is not a purely selfish exercise, though. To be a true accountability buddy, you need to be able to offer the same back to them. When my partner and I were working jobs we no longer found satisfying or rewarding, we agreed to become each other's accountability buddies to push each other to strive for more. This person should be someone who is trustworthy and who will be there for you when you doubt yourself and also when you succeed. If you can find this person and then, in turn, have the time and energy to help them also, then fantastic. As I said, it will help you in whatever it is you'd like to achieve. However, I don't believe you need to beat yourself up if you can't find this person or if you don't believe you can be of the same use back. An accountability buddy is a nice tool (one I've used to great success), but they are by no means a necessity. You will still achieve everything you want to on your own, as long as you can be accountable to yourself, and sometimes that requires you to get tough.

Getting tough with yourself

I want to open by saying that we aren't talking here about beating ourselves up whenever we make mistakes or when things don't work out. This isn't useful and won't help you to

BECOME ACCOUNTABLE

learn from your experiences. When I say 'tough', what I mean is having a serious look at your life and working out what you have been doing up to now that has prevented you from achieving or even going for what you want.

When I was younger and found myself lacking confidence, I didn't just sit in that for ever and accept that this was the way I was, that this was now my lot in life, to be a shy and quiet person. I realised that, if I ever wanted to achieve the things I wanted (friends, career, girlfriend, etc.), then I would have to do something about it. I'd have to find a way to adapt and change and then, yes, I got tough with myself. Being tough with yourself is realising it won't just magically happen, that you have to make a plan, you have to take action, you have to step outside of your comfort zone, you have to risk relationships and you have to be okay with failing. All tough things to accept.

Getting tough with yourself can transform your inner dialogue from a negative space into a positive one, and we can do this by creating an 'inner coach'. This concept of an inner coach means having a very supportive and motivational version of yourself in your head. Whenever it's time to do the hard work, we use our inner coach to get ourselves through it. Instead of the usual disempowering and critical thoughts, we can activate the inner coach by thinking positive internal thoughts about what we are experiencing: these can be empowering, and it's far more useful to our success and experience than berating ourselves. You can do this by asking yourself different out-of-the-box questions.

'Is the anxiety that's holding me back currently worth the pain of having the regret of not trying?'
'What am I really afraid of?'
'Will the scenarios I'm creating in my head actually come to fruition?'

These are the regular questions you should ask yourself, especially if you're prone to overthinking and anxiety. Your inner coach will be able to offer you a more realistic outcome. And sometimes you'll just have to talk yourself into doing something by simply taking action and making a move.

Sometimes you won't be able to talk down the anxious thoughts, however, and the only way for you to get past it will be to force yourself to do the thing you're anxious about. Once you take the first step, though, the others usually follow with ease. Give yourself reminders to push past the roadblocks in your mind. A great one I use regularly is that I remind myself of the fact that everyone who has ever achieved anything in their life had to do something they had never done before, and do you think they were scared the first few times? You bet they were! Success is found by doing the stuff you're scared to do, the stuff you've never done before. Telling yourself this and questioning your own unhealthy thought patterns regularly is what I mean by getting tough with yourself, and this will help you tremendously on your journey.

BECOME ACCOUNTABLE

Creating schedules

Part of being accountable to yourself is about keeping consistent. Anyone who can speak two or more languages will tell you that you have to practise the new language regularly for it to stick. Similarly, constant exposure to any new task will increase learning time and help you master whatever it is you want to achieve. Being consistent is not easy, though. You have to be disciplined, and a great way to help you stay disciplined is to create schedules for yourself.

A huge part of my success in the world of social media was down to being consistent. I always want to produce high-quality content, but sometimes it doesn't translate across – sometimes I just miss the message or package the content in the wrong way. Consistency is my method to make sure I don't let these setbacks deter me. I made a promise to post every day, regardless of how the last post was received. Having this schedule locked in means I can't dwell on failed attempts, and I have to keep on regardless. This is one of the single greatest things I did for my career and my content, and I thoroughly recommend it to anyone I meet now. Create a schedule for yourself as part of your timeline: put regular action points in your day or week, something you have to do, then keep that promise and stay accountable for yourself.

A schedule can look like doing something every day at a set time to help towards your goal or it might be a regular weekly fixture. I recommend starting small, though, as, like we said, you don't want to overdo it at the start by giving yourself too big a commitment and then burning out or becoming disillusioned about what you're trying to achieve. This would be a massive setback. It's a common misconception that we only get burned out from a life that we have little control of and a job we almost feel like we are forced to do, but the opposite is equally true. We can easily get burned out doing the stuff we love. If the schedule you've created to stay consistent is just too much – whether that's you start to hate it or it begins to stress you out – then scale it back a little. Find the amount of work required and how often it needs to be done for you to both find success and enjoy the process.

Mental health councillor LaShawnda McLaurin has this to say about consistency in her article, 'Consistency is Key': 'Read any book about success or listen to any story about someone's journey and you will hear about the importance of consistency. This is because anything worth having or doing takes a lot of time. Success is a marathon. Change is a marathon. These things take a long time to do, and thus you have to be consistent.'

I would add that I feel the best way to be consistent is to keep a schedule. You can buy cheap schedule planners online, you can put it in a calendar (physical or online), you can even write it in your Notes on your phone. I have a few daily reminders of what I need to do and when, and even after over three years of creating, I find these reminders to keep to my schedule invaluable.

We are all human, we can have off days, and by keeping to a

schedule you are putting the power back into your own hands. You are the one who has to get up and do the work, no matter how big or small, as no one else is here to do it for us, so tell yourself how you're going to do it. If you want this life, if you want these dreams, you have to become accountable for your life now and your future.

> When you're looking to create this schedule of yours, start small but be consistent with the planning, then add more difficult tasks as you get used to your schedule: we don't want to start too hard and fast and burn out, so to encourage success we will build up the schedule over time, making sure to include breaks, as rest is important for brain function and to avoid burnout. As you complete tasks in your schedule, take a moment to reward yourself too. These can be small things like actually telling yourself well done, but whatever you choose, rewards are important to help you stay motivated.

Celebrating success and rewards

The result of being accountable, taking your life seriously, making plans and then executing them is that your ambitions, what had started out as just dreams, are much more likely to become a reality. Sometimes this is an incredible feeling, but sometimes you don't even notice what you've done. For example, when I reached 100,000 followers on TikTok, I had been concentrating on the number and I had set it as a goal way before I even achieved 1,000 followers, so it was a happy moment for me for sure, but at the same time one of my goals was to change my life for the better, because of the doors having a large loyal following can open. My life has changed drastically for the better, but I never really took the time to process it as I was fixated on creating more. Yes, really, sometimes it just becomes a notch along the path to the bigger dreams and goals you've now set for yourself. So, there's an important step in all of this, and that's to actually celebrate your wins along the way and to reward yourself.

When I reached 100,000 followers on social media, I was shocked and giddy. I celebrated for the day, but that's all I allowed myself, because, before I knew it, I was at 250,000. My social media growth was unexpectedly rapid, and when I reached 1 million, I didn't feel anything and didn't do anything to mark the milestone. Looking back, I'm upset about this. I had become so used to the success that I couldn't even take a moment to be happy for myself, to take stock and notice what got me there. I just thought 'okay, great . . . what's next?' This mindset actually stunted my growth as a content creator because I just became accustomed to success and so dropped the ball a little. When you take the moment to stop, to feel real pride in yourself, and also find ways to reward yourself, you learn to value what you've achieved. Being happy and grateful in the present moment and celebrating all the things

BECOME ACCOUNTABLE

that have got you to this point (including your own hard work and dedication) will help build self-esteem and self-confidence.

Celebrating what you have achieved is also a great way to cement lessons you've learned as part of your journey. We talk about your timeline and your journey a lot in this book and part of that is celebrating your achievements. What's the point of doing any of it if we can't be happy in the high moments, especially as we have to ride so many down moments?

Harvard Business Review has this to say on celebrating small wins: 'Progress is hard-won early in a challenge (or task). It can be discouraging and require painful perseverance. So why wouldn't we celebrate the early victories, no matter how small? Celebrating small wins stimulates dopamine release in the brain, a feel-good chemical that reinforces the learning experience and strengthens our sense of connection to those we work with.'

In our case, most of this will be done alone, so we are reinforcing our connection with and building trust in ourselves. And high self-esteem will allow us to tackle more and gives us the faith to do good work in spite of even bigger obstacles. Find happiness in your success by taking stock, patting yourself on the back and rewarding yourself. It doesn't have to be anything gargantuan, but celebrate all of the wins and you will find true happiness in your timeline and process.

The building blocks of success

Accountability is one of the most important building blocks for success because, without it, you will always rely on the external for your sense of achievement and happiness, and in turn always blame the external for your failures. And if none of your dreams ever become a reality, there is the very real possibility that you'll feel you have a disappointing existence that makes you unhappy, disengaged and jealous of others. I know it's scary to realise you are in control of it all, that you have to hold the weight of it by yourself, but changing to this mindset of being responsible, taking action, learning from mistakes, building trust in yourself, becoming your own inner coach and creating an easy-to-follow schedule will get you to places you never thought possible before. And that's got to be worth the discomfort.

7
REJECT YOUR LAZY SIDE

'Alex, you're lazy.' I used to get this a lot, mostly from my mother and school teachers. They could see I had potential, they could see that all those years watching cartoons hadn't actually rotted my brain, but they just didn't understand why I didn't apply myself in relation to my education or at home. Now, as an adult, I'm seen as incredibly hard-working, probably even a little *too* hard-working. I bet at some point in your life you too have felt you were being lazy or someone else has told you that you were being lazy. But I'm about to change the way you look at this word, and propose how we can change the way we allow it to affect us, because guess what? There is no such thing as laziness.

What was seen by my teachers and parents was more than likely just a lack of enthusiasm about doing what I was told; I just didn't have any interest in the things I was supposed to be paying attention to. A lack of enthusiasm exists, but laziness does not. This lack of enthusiasm can have a positive effect on you *and* a negative one, but that all depends on whether you listen to what your enthusiasm is trying to tell you.

On one hand, your mind is telling you you'd rather be doing something else and that whatever you're dealing with doesn't align with your interests and purpose. This is fine when we come up against jobs that maybe we're not right for. This is your mind telling you this isn't for you and you need change. You're not lazy because you don't enjoy doing your job; it just doesn't feed into what's right for you, and your subconscious is trying to tell you that. This is a massive positive if we listen to it, because it means we can spark change. But we need jobs to live, to afford food and housing, so naturally we will stay in that job even though it doesn't fulfil us. But if we don't use our lack of enthusiasm as our spark for change, then we stay on but do the bare minimum to keep the job. To others, that might perhaps look like you being lazy, but it's not.

If you've got this far in the book, then you might be at a point in your life where things just haven't come together in the way you want them to. You want to achieve something but haven't done that thing yet. The idea of it or the pain point can be why you're thinking about it, why you're excited about the idea of change or excited about the results of this ambition, but you haven't got past the thought. Maybe you haven't started yet, or, even if you have, then maybe some of the work that is required you lack enthusiasm for. This can be for many reasons, and given how self-critical humans can be, a lot of the time a lack of action is characterised as laziness. So when this happens we have a tendency to overthink and believe we'll never achieve this dream because we think we're being lazy and that is demotivating and, ironically, keeps us in a funk. To get you going, we need to reject this notion that you're lazy, because you're not: you just don't have the enthusiasm for the task ahead and your energy for it is being damaged by your self-critical mindset.

What makes you give up

It is astounding how we all find ways to be so self-critical. In the past, I have told myself all sorts of unfounded lies in order to allow myself *not* to do something I know I should have really done. 'I'm not smart enough to do that job. I would actually be laughed out of the interview. If I don't actually go for it, then I'm protecting myself from the humiliation.'

This idea I had of myself, of not being smart enough, was completely made up, because I honestly wouldn't know either way unless I attempted it. But instead of trying, I chose my comfort zone and gave in to fear. This may be a familiar scenario for you: perhaps in the past (or even now) you have labelled yourself not good enough to attempt something, and so you haven't done it or don't even bother trying. And then the self-criticism comes for you in the aftermath and tells you you're lazy for not trying. Well, I'm here to tell you that you're not lazy, you're just scared. I was hiding from an unlikely humiliation, and you're probably doing the same now. We build these actions and decisions up so much in our head, but from my experience the reality is nowhere near as bad as what I've imagined.

We lack effort because of fear and then what was a nice idea for ourselves becomes a non-starter. We use excuses like it's 'too hard'. Something being too hard should no longer be an excuse for us. You can still accomplish it, no matter what. Forget failed attempts, forget humiliation, you're going to achieve this. You'll be laughing and celebrating in the end, and you can't be lazy if you are moving towards a goal, but the pace at which you do so is inconsequential.

> A brilliant way to handle these moments when you lack enthusiasm is to remind yourself of your pain points. Take out your notebook and write the answers to these questions: Why do you want this? What has happened or what is happening in your life right now that means you require this change? Circle your answers and copy them down in multiple places where you will see them: write them on the fridge or on your mirror, for example. These reasons and the ensuing answers are your weapon against any lack of enthusiasm.

You will always struggle to live a contented and happy life knowing that you could have done something about your life or situation but decided not to go for it because it was scary/

REJECT YOUR LAZY SIDE

too hard/outside of your skill set. Bullsh*t! You can accomplish anything if you reject your lazy side (whatever that may look like) and do not allow fear to dictate your effort.

What distracts you the most?

> 'Distractions destroy action. If it's not moving you towards your purpose, leave it alone.'
>
> JERMAINE RILEY

I am easily distracted; I'm currently being distracted right now. I've booked in at a lodge in the Peak District so that I can finish this book without my attention being stolen by everything that usually distracts me at home in London. And yet here, in this vast open countryside, I'm still distracted. There's a massive fly in the room and it's bothering me. My partner is going about her day and I just naturally like to stare at her. Plus, my phone is vibrating away with never-ending notifications. But the worst distraction is the bottle of wine I can see in the corner of my eye. This is my reward for today's writing, and it can't come soon enough. That's a distraction, but maybe a good one, as I need to know my reward is coming.

Distractions can be good or bad, and whether they are one or another depends entirely on if you use them to motivate you or if they are using you, and subsequently keeping you from your goals. An important lesson or step in achieving any goal you've never achieved before is to work out what each distraction is to you, good or bad. Is it helping you or is it hindering you?

Firstly, start with whatever the task is you're looking to achieve and then think of all the things that will distract you, and assess what will actually keep you from the goal. What will slow it down? And do you need it or not? These distractions are also not limited to things, as people can be an obvious distraction too. People we love, who we want to spend time with, so it's no fault of theirs that they can distract you, but sometimes they distract you in unsuspecting ways. For example, family members are part of your life and maybe certain people in your family rely on you to help them navigate their life, maybe some people need you to provide for them? These people can be time-consuming, which is a distraction when we are starting a new venture.

Another example can be your friends and social life, as while having some form of social life is good, because we can't be all work and no play (reasons for which I'll discuss in the importance of breaks section later in this chapter), but nevertheless they are still a distraction from this new ambition, which might be your priority now, but you will have to work out a way to go for your dreams and still manage your responsibilities in relation to them. Just don't use family as an excuse for not going for whatever you want. Many people have heavy responsibilities but still manage to create incredible things. If you really want this, you'll find a way to make it

REJECT YOUR LAZY SIDE

work. Find a way to prioritise them *and* your goals. Both will be important to you, so it's about finding the right balance.

Obviously, though, most people's biggest distraction is their phone. These annoying, fantastic, distracting little computers we keep in our pockets are indeed brilliant things. I've created a career using my iPhone, and that blows my mind in itself, but my phone equally slows down my work. The never-ending scroll, the constant contact with loved ones and the limitless entertainment options. I hate it and I love it. I need my phone for work, so I can't simply chuck it away, but I need to limit how much it distracts me. When financial TikTok creator Simon Squibb meets people in the street, he always tells them to delete all apps on their phone that don't align with their goals, claiming these are unnecessary distractions that will hinder their progress.

I have no games on my phone, I have no streaming services, I only have the social media platforms that I post on. Also, my phone is on Do Not Disturb the majority of the time, firstly because, as I said before, I get a lot of notifications and, secondly and more importantly, it gives me control of who gets my time and attention. A big modern-day problem is we are way too readily available, all the bloody time, because of our phones. By putting my phone on Do Not Disturb, it means I can check in and allow myself to be contacted at times that suit me. That way, I can get my writing and other work done. My phone is important to my work and life, but I put up barriers to stop it from distracting me and keeping me from reaching my goals. My phone is now a tool and not a hindrance.

So, what in your life is distracting you? Can you turn it into a tool, or will it always be a hindrance? That bottle of wine in the corner of my eye, for me, is actually a tool. If I was to crack it open now and drink and write, though, I imagine I'd write a load of crap. (You never know, I could be the next Hemingway, but it's far more likely the advice wouldn't be the best and there would be mistakes in my writing everywhere.) So, instead I use this distraction as a tool: the bottle has become a reward. Of course, this is not a daily reward, but I like a glass of wine and, if I tell myself that it is a distraction for me, but I don't get to touch it until I've written a few thousand words, then, you know what? . . . I'll get those words written. And if you need proof it works, here is the book, hopefully without too much crap in it!

This sounds a little more like a reward, but distraction and reward are inherently linked, as rewards are an important part of the creation process. As we discussed in Chapter 6 – Become Accountable, hard work without reward or celebration will stunt you. If you find yourself distracted easily, either because of a short attention span or due to a lack of enthusiasm, then as long as you believe deep within you that this is important work you need to do for whatever reason, you can use your distractions as rewards. You can scroll on your phone, but only after . . . You can eat that chocolate bar, but only after . . . You can go out and do the thing, but only after you've achieved your task, or whatever your timeline needs you to do this day.

Distractions are inevitable, so let's at least benefit from them, write down all the things, and potentially people, that

REJECT YOUR LAZY SIDE

distract you or that you believe will distract you. Work through each one and classify whether these are necessary to your life or not. If not, then look for ways to cut them out completely. If you deem the distraction as something you want to keep in your life, however, then you must turn it into a reward. You decide whatever work is required before you are allowed the distraction, and then, as long as you don't allow these distractions to derail you, they will lose some of their hold over you. When you put them behind an effort wall, these distractions will either become extinct or taste sweeter because of your hard work.

How to prioritise (i.e. the Snowball Effect)

There's something so unmotivating about taking on a task that seems like it will take a lot of time and effort. Usually this happens because there's so many parts to the task that need to be done in order to complete it. It's not just one thing, and your brain knows this. For example, you want to paint a room in your house. This task will require multiple jobs – going to the shop to buy paint, putting down sheets, taping the edges, all before you can actually get painting – and the thought of that can easily put you off the whole idea. So, when I'm faced with a task that seems like a lot of effort and time, a technique I use in these scenarios is called the Snowball Effect.

Many people believe, when you have a list of tasks to do,

that you should do the easiest one first. The idea here is that it gets you on track re completing tasks and motivates you for the next one on the list. This does work to some level, because the first step or experience usually takes some effort when attempting something for the first time, but where I have an issue with this approach is when one of the tasks is disproportionately harder in regard to difficulty and in terms of the level of effort that is required. Let's say you have six tasks: five easy ones and one big one . . . you complete the first five and pat yourself on the back for doing so, and you convince yourself that it's okay to leave the big task for another time, because, well, you smashed the day by completing the other five. This is quite obviously avoidance and will slow you down when it comes to growth and output because this approach will always have you avoiding the hard task. You have to bite the bullet by doing the hard task at some point, so my view is: why not attack it straightaway?

The Snowball Effect gets its name from the idea that a large snowball (big tasks), when rolled down a hill, will pick up more snow (more tasks) on its journey than a small snowball (easiest tasks), so doing the biggest, hardest task first will help you complete the whole task with far more efficiency. The idea is that we always attack the hardest activity or thing on our to-do list first, before anything else. We aim to do it before our unenthusiastic brain gets a chance to talk us out of it. The real beauty in doing this is how it makes you feel after you've tackled something you thought would be incredibly hard to do. You haven't avoided it, and you've made the difficult task the priority. Instead of patting yourself on the back after completing small tasks and then taking the day off, if you focus on completing the hardest first, it gives you true inspiration that you can do anything and then the motivation to ride rapidly through the smaller tasks. This also gives you the motivation to tackle bigger tasks in the future. Always take on the biggest, scariest, meanest task head-on and use that big snowball to swallow up the smaller snowballs.

Chunking (i.e. breaking down large tasks)

Maybe you've tried the Snowball Effect, or a form of it, before, and it hasn't worked for you, which is fair. Maybe the big task was a little too much or you had limited experience doing it and it overwhelmed you. Well, I'm going to give you a way to tackle those bigger tasks. It's called Chunking and I use it all the time when I have something pretty daunting to do.

In an article on Medium.com by Rode & Ankor about chunking they describe Chunking thus: 'Chunking is, at its core, a cognitive strategy that involves breaking down information into bite-sized pieces so the brain can more easily digest it.'

Think of it like eating. Instead of trying to eat an entire pizza in one go, you take bites to make consumption more manageable and efficient. Similarly, Chunking breaks a large task into a series of smaller steps or actionable tasks that make the overall project more digestible.

GET OUT OF YOUR OWN WAY

By taking a hard task and breaking it into smaller chunks, we help to eliminate the feeling of being overwhelmed by the task. Have you ever looked at a task and thought, 'Oh heck, where do I begin?' Chunking simplifies this and allows you to see this mountain of a task as a smaller, more manageable hill. It also allows you to see the process of completion with clearer vision, as you're virtually creating a road map of small tasks that need to be done, which means you can track your progress.

If you're anything like me and become a bit distracted and scattered by the big tasks, this will help you immensely. And it works in almost all scenarios. It's not possible to go to a gym to try and build an ideal body in a day or week; no, instead we chunk down workouts and, over a period of time, you'll complete that goal. It's unlikely we are able to write a whole book over a weekend, so instead we break down the chapters and headings and work on each section in their own right, and by the end of doing this you'll have yourself a book (as you can tell, my mind is rather focused on this one particular task right now . . .). You want to meet the love of your life but find it difficult to spark up conversations with strangers? Well, instead of telling yourself you have to meet them this week, you could work on yourself and find a way to be more socially confident, or work on your communication skills first, then try those skills out on some people you know better than a random stranger.

If it's unrealistic to take it all on in one go, break the task into these more manageable chunks. It's all about lots of little chunks that will, together, go towards achieving the final result.

REJECT YOUR LAZY SIDE

> So, when you are faced with any task that seems like a lot of work or potentially complicated, write it down and break the task into little chunks. Separate them until you think they are manageable and then take them on, one chunk at a time. All tasks can be broken down into different parts to make them more manageable.

How to incorporate affirmations and what effect it has on us

We spend so much time in our own heads (well, I do at least). Most of us have an ongoing dialogue that is constantly running through our head. Sometimes we hear and pay attention to this, but sometimes it passes by without us really concentrating on what our thoughts are saying.

Let's say you see a group of people playing volleyball: this is something you'd love to do, but you don't know them so you don't want to interrupt or get in the way. But wait, you haven't actually said this out loud; your anxious brain has managed to slip this thought into your mind and managed to talk you out of going over and seeing if you can join in without you even realising it. Without realising it, we take on these thoughts and adhere to them in our lives. Unfortunately, if you're an overthinker or prone to some anxiety, these thoughts are often not nice, helpful, productive or even true. We can say all sorts about ourselves. For example, 'I'm not confident enough to do that', with zero proof as to whether you are confident or not, or if you'd be interrupting their game. So many people suffer from negative brain chatter that it stunts us and doesn't allow us to attempt things we would like to do but never have. If we are forced to have this ongoing dialogue in our heads, then we need to start making it a happier, healthier place to be. And one way we can start doing this easily is with affirmations.

I have talked previously about catching negative thoughts, questioning them and testing their validity, but now we're going to actually force some positivity on ourselves. If our brains can believe untested negative suggestions about ourselves, then they can believe positive suggestions too. The power of this is actually quite astounding.

An article by psychologist and MBA Catherine Moore in *Positive Psychology* had this to say: 'There is MRI evidence suggesting that certain neural pathways are increased when people practice self-affirmation tasks [. . .] The results of a study by Falk and colleagues suggest that when we choose to practice positive affirmations, we're better able to view "otherwise – threatening information as more self – relevant and valuable".'

What this means is that when you tell yourself enough that you are capable of something, you will then believe you are capable of that thing. Whether or not you actually can do it is beside the point. What we want to do is genuinely believe we can so that we *do* go for it. When you genuinely believe with absolute confidence that you can do it, then you stop procrastinating and actually go for it. No more excuses, just action.

REJECT YOUR LAZY SIDE

So, to build incredible confidence with affirmations, you basically need to become your own personal cheerleader. Don't worry, I won't have you buying pompoms and doing backflips in the garden, but you should cultivate the peppy enthusiasm and the cheer to fill yourself with encouragement, and hopefully banish away the doubt.

> How we do this is, every day, a few times throughout the day, we will repeat some positive affirmations to ourselves. Write them down, if you want, and have them readily available to look at and recite. No more than six, and they should be personal to you: personal in a way that you feel something is lacking in your life and that has a connection to your ambitions and the journey you're on. If you're someone who has been limited in life by the belief in your own abilities, then you might say affirmations like: 'I am an incredibly confident person', 'I am deserving of my goals' and/or 'I will accomplish anything I set my heart out to do'. If you tell yourself this enough, you'll have the belief that you can do it.

I know that if you're not used to affirmations, it can be a bit awkward telling yourself that you're awesome, but the only way you'll find out is by trying it. Studies have proven it can decrease health-deteriorating stress and it's been used effectively in interventions that led people to increase their physical behaviour. Affirmations have also been linked positively to academic achievement by stopping Grade Point Average (GPA) decline in students who feel left out at college. And if you're someone, like me, who regularly comes up against low self-esteem because of your past, then has a constant negative dialogue in their head, this helps mitigate it at the source. Don't allow your fears and negative thoughts to stop you from going for everything you desire. Practice positive self-talk and see how much better you feel about everything.

Places/spaces and change of environment

I cannot work in a messy environment. I've also found I cannot work in a loud environment, and my ideas and creative capacity feel limited to what I can see in front of me. Often I have to find different places to create and work in if the current environment is not right for me. I love London and I love living there, and sometimes I find great inspiration in the city. However, a lot of the time I find it hard to think here. And when I'm finding it too distracting, I seek open spaces to create, which usually works instantly. I can be down and uninspired, but if I drive a few hours out to the countryside, I feel lighter. I find I can think more clearly and I genuinely feel like I'm more creative.

If you are born and raised in certain areas of the UK and

REJECT YOUR LAZY SIDE

US (and I'm sure this happens in other countries as well), the geographic location one is born in comes with pressure and/or judgement. People often succumb to their environments because going against what is normal for that environment is difficult. It invites judgement, as those around you say things like 'People don't do that around here', and then this can cause opportunities to close unless you assimilate. It's probably not the done thing to become the next big jazz musician if you live and were raised in Scunthorpe, which doesn't have a rich cultural history of jazz, for example.

Sometimes we need to break away from the shackles of our environments. If the environment you find yourself in currently doesn't help you grow, if it doesn't encourage your creativity or whatever you're looking to achieve, then a change of environment is important. You mustn't talk yourself out of not going for something you want because of your environment. Equally, you may be in the right place geographically but the space you're in doesn't help you. For example, in Hong Kong the price of rent is astronomical, so there's been a rise in closet rooms to rent. It's literally a room with a bed in it that's the size of a closet, and then a separate shared bathroom, yet the rent is still pretty steep. This allows people on a much smaller wage to live in Hong Kong. Hong Kong is a beautiful place and would definitely offer opportunities for growth and creativity, but I can't help but think if you're living in a closet room, and potentially working on something for you from that room, then the scope for creativity is severely limited to those four walls. Inevitably, your imagination becomes limited because of the lack of natural stimulation. While not impossible to still grow and create something incredible, if you find yourself in a similar situation then maybe it's time to look for a change of environment, especially if you've already tried to do it in your current environment with no success.

Your environment can also severely affect your mental health. A bad environment for you can raise your stress levels and increase feelings of anxiety and depression. In an article on VeryWellMind.com, mental health and fitness expert Sara Lindberg M.Ed discusses the impact our environments have on our mental health states: 'In some cases, environmental factors impact mental wellness by changing brain structure and function. Research on children supports this, noting that children raised in adverse environments tend to have hindered brain development, increasing their risk of memory issues, learning difficulties, and behavioural problems. Most notable factors include aesthetics, sensory, people, familiarity, culture and values.'

Most of us will experience positive and negative changes caused by our environment. What you need to work out is: does the current environment you find yourself in help you grow and go for what you want? Or does it stunt you? Think about what is best for your mental health going forward, because environments can change. You have a level of control here, and to use something that can be changed as an excuse for not going for your dreams would be wasted potential.

REJECT YOUR LAZY SIDE

> If you do require an environment change to help with growth or to just be more focused, then it will require you to test out different environments. Just because I enjoy working in outdoor spaces doesn't mean that will work for you. So, take your equipment and work out which places help you think more clearly and foster the most motivation.

The importance of breaks

In writing this chapter, I wanted to dissuade you from thinking you need to be going a hundred miles per hour all the time or tackle everything all at once to achieve your goals. Not going quickly doesn't mean you are lazy. Hopefully you've understood that how hard you attack this doesn't make a difference as long as you're not using certain excuses to not go for it. You also need to have a plan of action and ensure that you are using the best methods for you to achieve that goal.

And one final thing I want to add, to even further prove that I am not endorsing speeding through tasks, is that regardless of the pace you are going and how often action is required, it is incredibly important that you take breaks away from your goals.

An article in *Forbes* magazine by Stuart R. Levine titled 'Rest For Success' states: 'Perpetual movement without rest decreases productivity. In reality, it yields the opposite. Working without downtime reduces efficiency and creativity and often invites emotional, psychological, and physical stress. The brain needs downtime to remain productive.'

This feels almost impossible in today's fast-paced life, where it incorrectly feels like we should be instantly successful in whatever venture we attempt. This becomes particularly emphasised if you're excited about what you're trying to achieve, or you've become desperate to reach completion because of what you will gain from the results. But working without breaks is unhealthy. Start telling yourself that taking regular breaks does not make you lazy, in fact it helps with creativity and productivity. Albert Einstein, one of the most creative minds we've ever known, regularly scheduled in quiet time for himself. His biographer, Walter Isaacson, related how Einstein would spend hours alone thinking; he would take himself off for long walks or sail on his boat. The quiet in both these activities allowed for creative thoughts and he would often find himself being able to answer difficult equations that he couldn't resolve before.

So, when you're planning out your day, do not shy away from breaks, from a few hours a day to weeks at a time. It doesn't matter, as it is all part of your process. Forcing the work will only push you back or have you create something you're not happy with. And, also, find different ways to take breaks, because one person's idea of a break can look different to another's. I personally appreciate quiet time alone and mindfulness meditation, but then sometimes I find my brain feels rested, rejuvenated and motivated by social gatherings. Do your best to keep the break and your work separate. If your work is in a certain place, then go somewhere that doesn't make you

REJECT YOUR LAZY SIDE

think of that place, or if you can take your work anywhere, then take on an activity as your break that is entirely separate and consumes you in enjoyment. Find your peace and schedule it in regularly, because it's all part of your journey.

8
BUILD SELF-ESTEEM WHEREVER POSSIBLE

A dangerous human is someone that is unbelievably comfortable with themselves, someone who knows who they are and are proud, someone who has the confidence to attempt anything, who has the confidence to believe they will succeed in everything they attempt, who is happy and content and does not sway from their ideals, beliefs and self-esteem in spite of what others say. The majority of people do not have this sorted, and so do not possess these attributes, and that means they are either drawn to the actual dangerous humans, or they fear them. Most people don't like seeing others with this much power, because it makes them jealous, as these people can do things that they can't. And while some might reject these anomalies, others find themselves pulled into their aura and can't seem to control their feelings. Human beings find comfort in normality, in the status quo, and rejecting (or, in this case, ascending beyond) the standard way of thinking is thought of as dangerous, because it is challenging the standard way of doing things, and many are threatened by that. But, to achieve great things, we need to become, or at least aspire towards becoming, dangerous humans. So this is the blueprint.

How to build self-esteem

> 'In reality, other people liking you is a bonus. You liking yourself is the real prize.'
>
> ALEX ELLE

Self-esteem can equally be called self-confidence, but in a nutshell it is how we feel about, value and perceive ourselves. Having healthy levels of self-esteem is one of the greatest ways to feel content in life, and to have the confidence to go for our life goals, and it can give you a sense of belonging and makes you feel secure. Having low self-esteem will have you questioning everything about yourself, from your looks to your ability to achieve or attempt something. Low self-esteem will have you making life choices based on other people's opinions because you're not sure of your own opinion/thoughts or because you prioritise other people's preferences as you see them as more important than your own. It will inevitably lead you to make

BUILD SELF-ESTEEM WHEREVER POSSIBLE

life choices for yourself that are below what you are capable of, because you lack belief in what you think you can achieve.

It is incredibly important to raise your self-esteem so that you can think further out of the box, so you can achieve things you've only dreamed of, and so you have the genuine confidence to know that you can, and that all will be okay, because it's you, and you've got this.

In an article on Very Well Mind, Kendra Cherry, MSEd, describes having good self-esteem as: 'You probably have healthy self-esteem if you: avoid dwelling on past negative experiences. You believe you are equal to everyone else, no better and no worse. You express your needs. You feel confident. Have a positive outlook on life, you say no when you want to, and you see your overall strengths and weaknesses and accept them.'

These are all healthy and strong mental attributes to have, and having high self-esteem can help you to reach your goals because you have the inner belief that you can take on most that life throws at you.

There are a few good things we can do to raise our self-esteem:

> 1. Inner validation: we spend so much of our lives trying to impress people, trying to impress our parents and teachers, friends, peers and colleagues – the list goes on. But how about instead of looking for that 'atta boy' or other term of validation from someone else, you give it to yourself. Start by telling yourself how

incredibly well you're doing so far: you're alive and kicking, and you are who got you here, so tell yourself well done. Anytime you do anything outside of your comfort zone, congratulate yourself. It's hard, it's uncomfortable, and yet you kept pushing yourself for better. Buy yourself something pretty, or tell yourself you are deserving and you're on the right path. You must not seek external validation, you must not do things for others, you must not do things to impress others; you can be proud, but you really don't want to show off. You're doing this for you and only you can tell you that you are enough.

2. Do not compare yourself to others: as we discussed in Chapter 1 – Acknowledge and Design Your Own Timeline, you are on *your* journey, and they are on *theirs*. People will be ahead of you and more successful, and others will be behind, but none of it matters: this is your journey, and you should be going for things in your life because you want them and not because others have them.

3. Catch the negative self-beliefs: anything you think negatively about yourself, catch it, look for the holes in the thought, and then replace it with a positive. Constant negative self-chatter will impact you negatively and prevent you from believing in yourself. It's only natural, and this will happen, but these negative thoughts have no proof, and the good news is we can make our brain believe the opposite by filling it with

BUILD SELF-ESTEEM WHEREVER POSSIBLE

tons of positive self-beliefs. Instead of thinking 'no one likes me', 'I can't do this' and 'what's the point?', we should change our inner dialogue to 'I am loveable', 'I am capable' and 'I can do whatever I put my mind to'.

4. Write down all your strengths and then write down all of your weaknesses because everyone has both, even dangerous humans. The difference is that highly confident people with healthy self-esteem love their strengths – they praise themselves for them, use them regularly – but they also understand and forgive their weaknesses. They know that no one can be perfect, so accept the parts of themselves that aren't. That doesn't mean they won't work on their weaknesses, but it's more that they don't let the negatives stop them. As with failure, weaknesses are a place to learn, grow and improve. An opportunity rather than a hindrance.

5. Handle other people, strangers and those very close to you: the best way to do this is by setting healthy boundaries. Start by asking yourself what you like and what you don't. What can you tolerate and what has a negative effect on your mental health? And then calmly communicate those boundaries to those who need to hear them. Healthy boundaries are key for strong connections with others. You believe you are worthy of respect, and communicating this to others and potentially cutting people out who do not believe you are worthy of that same respect will give you more self-belief.

> 6. Taking risks: potentially incredible success is on the other side of the risk. By actioning the advice I've given you in this book, you are taking that risk. You want more, and you'll realise quickly you are capable of more because you show yourself that you can handle it, and the more you take these risks and surprise yourself, the higher your self-esteem and confidence builds.

Practise all these things above and watch your self-esteem build. I'd recommend you keep a self-esteem journal, where you can keep note of all the times you do these six things, and hopefully keeping them close to you and written down will help to remind you of how it's important to action these whenever you can. The higher you can build your self-esteem, the more likely you will find yourself achieving incredible feats in your life.

How to practise self-love

Self-love is the act of looking after yourself, physically and mentally. Not treating yourself like a human garbage can but as something rare and valuable. The art of self-love is to start taking care of *you*.

Let's start with sleep. Sleep was something I never cared for

BUILD SELF-ESTEEM WHEREVER POSSIBLE

much as a teenager or even in my twenties. Lots of late nights and early starts had me not getting the adequate amount of sleep regularly. And sleep has a massive effect on my mental health; I am nowhere near the confident, happy person I can be when I haven't had the right amount of sleep, and that's not to mention how emotional it can make me too.

An article written by Eric Suni for The Sleep Foundation about the link between our mental health and sleep states: 'Brain activity fluctuates during sleep, increasing and decreasing during different sleep stages that make up the sleep cycle. Each stage plays a role in brain health, allowing activity in different parts of the brain to ramp up or down and enabling better thinking, learning, and memory. Research has also uncovered that brain activity during sleep has profound effects on emotional and mental health.'

It's quite simple: get a sufficient amount of sleep and you will perform better in all aspects of your life, decrease anxiety and limit depression, as well as feel better about yourself and overall be more confident. And you can do this by practising better sleep habits. Start by creating a set bedtime and maintaining that sleep schedule. Of course, this won't always be possible, but the more regular a bedtime you have the better. It's also important to wind down before bed. Try some relaxation techniques, like reading or meditation, and do this every night for one hour or even just 30 minutes before your bedtime. And keep your phone away from your eyes and ears during this period. Our phones energise us, stimulate us and can induce anxiety, and you don't want this just before bed. And, finally, try to avoid alcohol too close to bedtime, and block out any excess light and sound that could disrupt sleep. By taking these simple steps, before you know it you'll be sleeping like a baby and surfacing the next morning with a clearer and happier outlook.

Another big part of loving yourself is what you consume. If you drink alcohol heavily, and have a poor diet of processed and fast foods, you're naturally going to feel like sh*t. The old saying of 'you are what you eat' is true: what you put into you will come out in more ways than one, and your mental health is a huge part of that. Now, I'm no party pooper, and I like a drink, and I like a takeaway pizza even more, but it's all about moderation and balance. Look to incorporate a Mediterranean diet into your life, as this has the best balance, and then watch the change in your mental health and physical health when you do.

The Mediterranean diet is often considered healthy because it emphasises whole, nutrient-dense foods and limits processed and refined foods, which are often high in unhealthy fats, added sugars and salt.

Healthline conducted a small, 12-week 2022 study of 72 men, ages 18 to 25, with moderate to severe depression, comparing the Mediterranean diet to befriending therapy (a modality that involves introducing a patient to at least one other person in the hope of providing them with more social support). The study found that the participants who followed the Mediterranean diet reported better quality of life than the group who received befriending therapy. The reason for these results is

BUILD SELF-ESTEEM WHEREVER POSSIBLE

arguably down to the fact that fresh fruits and vegetables have vitamins, minerals and fibre, which boost brain function. Fibre regulates blood pressure, which may aid in reducing anxiety and depression. Omega-3 fatty acids may boost mood and lower inflammation, while improved gut health can affect mood.

I understand that no diet can be perfect and nor can one person. Enjoy your life and find times to indulge, but it has been scientifically proven that sticking predominantly to a healthier, balanced diet will improve you physically and mentally. When you put goodness into you, you will project goodness back – for example with clearer, positive and more confident thinking patterns. When you are feeding yourself good-quality food and drink, you are showing respect for yourself, and this is the ultimate offering of self-love. Look after you and you will be rewarded.

And, lastly, my favourite way to practise self-love is to exercise and spend time outdoors, in nature. And if you can incorporate the two of them at once, then even better. I spent most of my life never really exercising. I did in school, but then from 16 till about 27 I did nothing. I didn't realise the effect it was having on me until I started going to the gym at 27. When I started, I almost instantly felt better about myself: it gave my day some routine and, with that, I started to watch what I was consuming. Your body notices when you are taking care of it and will reward you with dopamine.

I do understand, though, that exercising can be tough and time-consuming, and if you haven't done it for a while, it's incredibly daunting. I've mentioned this already, but being a novice and having to enter somewhere like a gym with so many seasoned pros about can be anxiety-inducing, so it's not an easy step to take. However, it's never as bad as you make it out to be in your head, and when you start doing it regularly, it has an incredible effect on the way you look at yourself. When you get in better physical shape, you are proving to yourself that you respect yourself. It's also an accomplishment to be in good shape, so when you do so, and then congratulate yourself for putting in the work, your self-esteem takes a boost.

I would recommend doing some research into different types of exercises and trying different ones. I'm personally not a fan of running, as I'd rather lift weights or go for walks, but find what works for you. I won't bore you with the science, but hundreds of studies have found a positive link between exercise and mental health. And by finding an exercise that's right for you, you're looking after yourself mentally *and* physically.

I also mentioned about getting some time outdoors in nature, and if you can link it with exercise, then that's brilliant. Not all exercise has to be lifting weights or long-distance running, as you don't have to go hard to stay in shape. Simply inserting walks into your week is equally important. Any level of physical movement is already tons better for you than doing nothing. But why is nature so incredible for showing love to yourself?

Leading mental health group Mind has this to say in an article about the connection between nature and our mental health: 'Spending time in nature has been found to help with

BUILD SELF-ESTEEM WHEREVER POSSIBLE

mental health problems such as anxiety and depression. For example, research into ecotherapy (a type of formal treatment which involves doing activities outside in nature) has shown it can help with mild to moderate depression.' (© Mind. This information is published in full at mind.org.uk)

The benefits don't end there either. Being outdoors can improve your mood, reduce feelings of stress or anger quickly, and even help reduce loneliness. I often take moments outdoors and reflect on how incredible nature is, and I love how small it makes me feel. Sometimes we get so wrapped up in our problems and get overly stressed, and the vastness and beauty of nature can make you realise how insignificant the thing you were stressing about is.

All of these things are incredible ways of practising self-love. And if you look after yourself in these ways, there's a good chance your mental health will improve, and then in turn improve you, allowing you to have higher self-esteem, greater confidence and then the ability to go for your wildest goals. The only thing I will add is: don't wait until you have high self-esteem to go for it. Build self-esteem and look after yourself while you're on your journey and while you're experiencing new things.

GET OUT OF YOUR OWN WAY

How confidence actually works
(i.e. action before belief)

> 'The actions of confidence come first; the feelings of confidence come later.'
>
> RUSS HARRIS

For the majority of my life, I believed I couldn't go to that social event, I couldn't go speak to that girl I liked, I couldn't ask for what I wanted, because I knew I didn't have the confidence to do it. I would see friends and peers do the things I wanted and just assume that they had the confidence, and that they must have just been born with it. These things I wanted to do were simply not going to happen because of the way I was raised and the trauma from my childhood, meaning I would only have small amounts of confidence in certain things (like sports), and I'd just never have it in other things. It wasn't until I saw the Russ Harris quote above that I really thought about confidence as a construct. Only when I broke down what confidence was did I finally understand:

> Dictionary.com definition of *Confident*: sure of oneself; having no uncertainty about one's own abilities, correctness, successfulness

BUILD SELF-ESTEEM WHEREVER POSSIBLE

No one, and I mean *no one*, can be absolutely, with no uncertainty, confident that they will succeed in something. You would have to be delusional to believe this, as there is always a chance that you will fail. That is, except for one thing: you've done it before!

There it was: the answer . . . standing there, almost mocking me . . . *experience*. Anyone who is the dictionary definition of confidence in anything has had experience; they have done it before and succeeded, so they know they can and probably will succeed again. You do not have confidence *before* the action, you only feel confident *after* taking the action. You then have the confidence to do it again, even if you failed, as you know what you did wrong, know that you're still here, and that you are capable of trying again. So you may not be confident you will succeed, but you will be confident enough to try. And that really is the only way to succeed: to try.

This was a game-changer for me. It allowed me to attempt absolutely anything I was scared to do, knowing that it is normal to feel fear, knowing that anyone else who also had no experience in an activity would also feel the same. So, yes, I would never have the confidence to do the action, unless, that is, I actually tried it. This opened up doors, windows, everything for me. And I hope it will help everyone else too, as they realise they have the potential to do anything. The only difference is some will never go for it because they are waiting to feel confident *before* they start.

Start and you will gain the confidence later.

The difference between confidence and arrogance

Having confidence and being a confident person is fantastic: you stand taller and feel pride in yourself because you have faith in your abilities. Confidence makes anyone more attractive and it's one of the top three traits most look for when finding a partner or hiring someone for a job. The more confidence you have, the more likely you are to live a happier, more successful life, and you do this (as we discussed in the last section) by experiencing and going for lots of new things that you would normally fear.

However, confidence has an ugly brother: arrogance. Arrogance will typically be found in the top three traits of what people do *not* want in a partner or employee. The problem is that confidence and arrogance are very similar, and often people mistake one for the other. It's important to be a confident person, but you need to be very careful not to become arrogant. So let's explore the difference.

The best way to tell them apart is that a confident person has a genuine sense of self-worth that doesn't need external validation. They are aware that they may not be perfect and may not know everything and they are okay with that, because they have the self-belief that they can learn and be open to new opinions and experiences. Arrogance, however, can be seen as an inflated sense of self-importance and superiority; these people generally believe they are better than everyone else and love to show that off. Arrogant individuals often exaggerate

BUILD SELF-ESTEEM WHEREVER POSSIBLE

their abilities, achievements or knowledge so they can show dominance over others.

One of the biggest differences between confidence and arrogance lies in how a person with each of these will go about interpersonal relationships. Confident people will be approachable, as they want to converse, share ideas, listen to others, value others and collaborate. They recognise that other people's perspectives can lead to better outcomes, potentially for a better result than just going with their own thoughts and opinions. Confident people have a self-assuredness that allows them to accept feedback and learn from their mistakes and failures. In contrast, arrogant people tend to struggle to connect with others on commonality. They may be dismissive, sometimes condescending, or uninterested in others' ideas or opinions (again, drawing their strength only from a comparison with and frequently belittling of others). This can lead to a breakdown of relationships, whether that's professional or personal. It's hard to get along with someone who always thinks they're right and doesn't really care for your opinion.

Confidence is inward-facing – it helps you believe internally you are capable of doing something, without any external factors getting involved. Confidence can do a task (or believes it can do it) without thinking of others. Arrogance is usually outward-facing, in that while arrogance believes they can do something too, it is very much reliant on comparison to others. It wants to succeed in relation to others and its sense of its confidence is more a feeling of superiority that comes only from being better than those around it.

Fake it till you make it (how it works and doesn't work)

You may have already heard of the concept of 'faking it till you make it', but if you haven't, then the idea behind it is to act as if you *are* something even if you feel as if you're not, and then keep doing this until you do eventually *become* that thing. So, with confidence, we act that way until we actually become confident. This theory does in fact divide opinion, with some saying it works while others believe that it doesn't make you whatever you want to be and that you'll just be acting as someone you're not, which can be a problem in itself.

You might, for example, run a risk of biting off more than you can chew, in that you may talk yourself into a situation that you really did need some experience for and, without it, you hypothetically drown and set yourself back. And while we should be okay with making mistakes, this is not really ideal.

I personally believe the upside of faking it does outweigh the bad sides, especially when it comes to confidence. As we've discussed before, the action and experience of something will make you confident after, not before. So, for example, if you want to build some kind of business venture for yourself, offering some kind of service, you have to start somewhere and you can't always start with experience. Yes, you can practise, but to make it a viable business, you need customers. This is where, at the start, you will have to fake it and act as if you know exactly what you're doing, even if you will be learning

BUILD SELF-ESTEEM WHEREVER POSSIBLE

as you go. And some mistakes may be made, but you can learn and then find ways to handle them in the moment. This is essentially the only way to build the experience you need.

To be confident in anything you will have to experience it, and you'll give yourself better odds of success by acting like you know what you're doing before you do. Everyone has to start somewhere, and you're not born with the experience: sometimes you have to be an imposter to become a master. Every big leap and then subsequent achievement in my life came from putting myself out there and doing something I didn't know how to do. I would often exaggerate my skills when applying for certain roles or jobs, as this helps you to get work you otherwise previously wouldn't be able to, although it does leave you in the deep end and having to learn or adapt those skills quickly. But I'd rather push myself to do something I've never done and then teach myself as I went along than sit on the outside wondering 'what if?' And once I reach the point of having learned what I needed to, this then made me more and more confident, as it can with you.

You're trying to build something new for yourself here. You're looking to expand outside of the normal version of yourself. You're sick of your comfort zone and want to experience the things you've only ever thought about. This is a scary process, but something needs to change in order for whatever you want to happen to come about. This will require bravery, and if you fake bravery when you're scared, then that *is* bravery.

So, yeah, my advice . . . fake it till you make it.

Daily habits that can make you confident

What we've discussed so far has probably got you thinking: 'Great, I understand I have to push myself; I understand I need to step outside of my comfort zone and take action. But how the heck do I do that?' We've already discussed leaning on your pain points to help push you or finding inspiration from your newfound self-esteem, but you might still need a little push and, lucky for you, I have a few activities and exercises that you can do that will help boost your confidence. These actionable tips will help you feel better about yourself and are known to boost dopamine. They are all things that I started a while ago on my quest to be more confident and, when done consistently, I can say they have been life-changing for me. You'll even feel the boost from the first time you try them, so what are you waiting for?

The one I always get the most resistance on when I share these tips, but is definitely my favourite, is cold water immersion. It was made popular by people like Wim Hof, but has been a practice for hundreds of years.

Wim describes it like this in his book, *The Wim Hof Method*: 'Cold Water Immersion (CWI) is a form of cold water therapy, which improves the natural recovery process of the human body.'

It has been reported that CWI can activate the body's natural healing powers by relieving symptoms of many health conditions, the one I'm most interested in being the suggested improvements to our cardiovascular health.

BUILD SELF-ESTEEM WHEREVER POSSIBLE

How you choose to do your own Cold Water Immersion is entirely up to you. A few of my close friends have bought barrels to immerse themselves in freezing-cold water and one even just swims in the sea in winter (yes, he's a madman!). I, on the other hand, have found that simply having a cold shower gives me the benefits, and even then, if you're still struggling with that, you can have a hot shower but for the last 30 seconds of the shower, just turn it to cold, start there, and as you get more accustomed to it, then build up to a minute, two minutes, and then a whole shower.

The key scientific benefit here is enhanced circulation of the blood. While there are other benefits, I find this one the most useful, because this will increase your energy levels and help balance your mental health. Me and my close friends discuss regularly the mental boost this gives us. It is almost like a natural high; it makes you feel powerful, less anxious and, in turn, more confident. Try to make this a consistent habit or do it on days where you have to do something you're pretty anxious about. You'll feel an instant confidence boost.

Another activity I implore you to take up, and which will also make you feel more confident, is to cut out complaining from your daily life. Life will ebb and flow, and you'll have great days and terrible days: this will happen naturally and there's not a lot we can do about it. For example, it rains the moment you leave the house, you get stuck in a traffic jam when you're in a rush, the supermarket runs out of eggs and all you wanted was to make an omelette. These are all minor inconveniences in the grand scheme of things. When these things happen to you, it is crucial that you react in a certain way. The reason for this is we don't want to start a consistent 'victim' inner dialogue. The problem is that when you think of yourself in this light, it is damaging to your mental health as you're telling yourself you have no control. Especially when things like this happen regularly, the constant negative mood will put you in a negative mindset. This is not a good breeding ground for belief, growth or confidence.

Travis Bradberry, Ph.D., wrote in an article on Talant Smart, EQ, and he proposed the following: 'Repeated complaining rewires your brain to make future complaining more likely. Over time, you find it's easier to be negative than to be positive, regardless of what's happening around you. Complaining becomes your default behaviour, which changes how people perceive you.'

In general, most of us don't like to be around negative people who complain all the time. If you are around this mindset regularly, there is a danger you could adopt it, and that's why you and everyone else doesn't love negativity. So, while it is important to talk about what is troubling you, you put yourself at risk of alienating yourself from people you care about or stunting yourself from creating new friendships and relationships by being negative all of the time.

The problem as well is it's not just how others perceive you, it's how *you* perceive you! The more you complain, the more negative you naturally are, and then, in turn, you are far less likely to start a new experience or, if you do, then you are highly likely to give up after a negative setback. You will

BUILD SELF-ESTEEM WHEREVER POSSIBLE

always experience these mundane annoyances in life and, if you manage to take them on the chin and not complain about them, then you are taking back control over them. You're telling the world that this doesn't affect you, this won't knock you off your stride. This will have you feeling far more positive about life, far more confident, and positive, confident people tend to be far more successful in this life.

The last daily tip I have that I want you to try is not to go on your phone when you first wake up. That's not to say you can't look at it later and throughout the day, but I'd recommend leaving it for the first hour after you wake up. A lot of the content you would be looking at on your phone is anxiety-inducing, as seeing other people show off their fantastic life on social media and that they are on their grind, say, will have you instantly comparing yourself, and this is the last thing you want when you first wake up. Even if you like to read the news, it's designed to make you feel cautious and wary. This is not the state of mind you want when you first wake up. As humans we tend to start as we mean to go on. If you start the day anxious and in a bad mood, then the day will continue like that, as negativity breeds negativity. So, with that thought, I want you to start your day with a happy, positive and powerful mindset. With that first 20 minutes you usually use to scroll on your phone, I want you to do something that will develop *you* instead. Read some non-fiction, exercise, plan, meditate. Anything that is known to put you in a better mental state, and then your day will continue in the same vein. You'll be far more confident and positive throughout your day and that attitude will help push you out of that comfort zone.

Understanding confident body language and the trick it has on our consciousness

Our brains are easily tricked and we're not so intelligent as we might think. This may sound quite hard to hear, but it's a good thing, especially when it comes to confidence. As with faking it till we make it, when you start to do something or be something regularly, our brains will over time believe we actually are what we are pretending to be, and one incredible thing you can do to trick your brain into thinking you're more confident than you are is to use confident body language.

When we walk, sit and take up space with confident body language, a message is sent to our brain that we are comfortable and confident in our surroundings, and this helps reduce anxiety. Thankfully, you don't need to stand there in a Superman pose (although that would still work); it can be much more subtle than that.

> So, I suggest you practise simply standing taller, and keeping your spine upright when you're walking and sitting. Keep your head up when walking, in social settings, and keep your chest open and try not to cross

BUILD SELF-ESTEEM WHEREVER POSSIBLE

> your arms or have your hands in your pockets. Take up more space when you're sitting: find a balance, and don't diminish your space at the expense of others. But there's no need for man spreading either, though I like to extend my arms when I'm sitting. Try your best not to fidget or be on your phone in public situations.

To others, doing all this will suggest you are a confident person and, to yourself, you're telling your brain you are in control, and you can be at ease. To others, this will make you appear comfortable in the environment, approachable and open.

Arlin Cuncic of Very Well Mind suggests this in their article on building inner confidence: 'Even if you don't feel confident, practising confident body language can increase your self-esteem and help you feel better about yourself.'

The one that the majority of people struggle with most is holding good eye contact. Holding eye contact can feel intense, and when you have a lack of self-esteem, eye contact can make you very self-aware. Ideally you want to look anyone in the eye when you're talking to them: hold it for more than a few seconds, look away for a second, and then look back into their eyes. This is good eye contact, as you don't want to be staring at the floor or have your eyes darting all over the place since this makes people feel uneasy because you seem unconfident and, in turn, you will feel unconfident. When we can't hold someone's eye when talking to them, we're telling our brain that this person is superior to us, and we are not confident enough to interact with them. This is not what you want from any interaction, whether it's social or professional. Holding good eye contact isn't about feeling more superior to anyone else either, but being able to hold it shows you are equals and this is where you want to be. If you build your self-esteem, you won't feel like there's a power imbalance and you'll feel equal, and this then affords you the confidence to hold good eye contact.

> In the meantime, I want you to practise. As always, start small with small amounts of eye contact until you feel comfortable, and then work your way up to longer and longer stints. Also, you want to be aware that you're not staring, as this is different to good eye contact, and this is why we take small breaks away from the eyes while talking and listening.

Practise all of these confident body language actions and feel the change for yourself. Be confident in yourself because you're doing incredible work: stand tall, keep your head up, look everyone in the eye and smile as much as you can.

BUILD SELF-ESTEEM WHEREVER POSSIBLE

The power of mindfulness and meditation

Mindfulness is a way of paying attention to the present moment without adding judgement or overthinking it. It's known to help people become more aware of their thoughts and feelings and so can help us cope with difficult thoughts and feelings. One type of mindfulness is meditation and its goal is to help you to become hyperfocused on what you're sensing and feeling in the moment. The practice of mindfulness mostly involves breathing methods and guided imagery to relax the body and mind, and this in turn helps reduce stress and catches any unwanted thoughts or feelings.

The website Mindful states the benefits of mindfulness meditation as: 'You become more aware of your thoughts. You can then step back from them and not take them so literally. That way, your stress response is not initiated in the first place.'

How you practice this is up to you. I started out by using mindfulness meditation apps like Headspace, but there are tons of others and free courses on YouTube as well. I felt a guided mediation, to start with, really helped me to focus on the activity and get into it. Most are between five- and 30-minute sessions and after it becomes a habit, you'll be able to do your own ones without being guided.

The key here is the power it gives you to catch your thoughts and this allows you to identify and catch negative ones and turn them into more of a positive one, or at least stop it affecting you as much. Before I discovered mindfulness, I was completely unaware of how much negativity was festering in my mind. I was being unconfident and believing in the fear I was feeding myself. We will only be as confident as our mind allows us to be, so use mindfulness to weed out the negative and then make a conscious effort to fill yourself up with positive thoughts that will only help you.

The link between gratitude and overall happiness

> 'Happiness is a journey, not a destination.'
>
> ALFRED D. SOUZA

I've spent my whole life seeking new ways to be happy. I'd say to myself things like: 'I'll be happy when I achieve this' or 'I'll be happy if this happens', only to find that, when those things happened, I was only happy for a few moments and then went back to wondering why I wasn't happy all the time. And as this made me feel incomplete, I would then look to the next thing that would make me happy.

This is evident in what is known as the Holiday syndrome. You are not content with your day-to-day life so you book a holiday (vacation for you, my American friends). You get super

BUILD SELF-ESTEEM WHEREVER POSSIBLE

excited about this holiday because it's everything you don't have in your normal life. But sometimes you get on that holiday and you still don't feel completely happy. Maybe it's not quite what you were expecting, maybe you put too much pressure on yourself to have a good time, or maybe you love it but you're anxious the whole time because, in a week or two, you've got to go back to work. This is no way to live and you'll always be chasing something else, asking yourself 'What's next?' This cycle will never end.

The moral of the story is achieving what you've always wanted in life will make you happy, but it will more than likely be short-lived. So, when we are assessing what we want from life and how we go about it, the reasoning for wanting it should not be to make us happier, as this suggests we aren't happy now and that only this thing or this achievement will get us to happiness. No, we want to work out a way to be happy with who we are and what we have but also be interested in personal growth. If we are able to be happy in the present, then we will be equally as happy with the results of growth. What we are really doing by achieving everything we've always wanted is building our self-esteem and creating a platform for our future, setting ourselves up for new adventures and opportunities we would more than likely never have a chance of experiencing, and which we may even have never known we wanted. True happiness and contentment is in the now and the ability to grow.

So, before we can add happiness from our growth and achievements, we must find our happiness in the now, and this is where gratitude comes in. Happiness in what you already have, and what you are experiencing today. Whether you're in your office job or on holiday, each day has something or a few things you can be grateful for and then find happiness in.

> 'Be grateful, for gratitude can bring life to life, it can turn a meal to a feast, resentment to love, a grudge to forgiveness, an enemy to a friend, a disease to hope and you to enough.'
>
> STEVEN BARTLETT, *HAPPY SEXY MILLIONAIRE: UNEXPECTED TRUTHS ABOUT FULFILMENT, LOVE AND SUCCESS*

I was incredibly lucky to have a mother who worked in the airline industry, so as a family we were able to afford cheap air travel and accommodation around the world. Even on a small wage, my mum was able to offer me and my siblings regular holidays. I sat in first class to Buenos Aires at the age of 12 and sailed on catamarans in Antigua when I was 15, all the time thinking this was pretty normal and yet still finding ways to be unhappy. I would look back at those times as an adult and think I didn't realise how good I had it. When I was a younger man and started paying for my own vacations, I soon realised the difference, but I was happier on those less exotic holidays with my knees up to my ears in economy on a flight to Tenerife because I was proud that I had actually worked for

BUILD SELF-ESTEEM WHEREVER POSSIBLE

it. I had got myself a job and I worked hard in it and for long enough to afford a holiday abroad. I was happy because I was thankful that I had a job and thankful for myself.

So now, whenever I find myself feeling a bit down, I start to look for what I can be grateful for and my joy quickly comes back. I think about how hard I've worked and how far I've got with my content. I think about how I was able to buy my first home this year. I think about how lucky I am to be here when so many are not. I think about how lucky I am to have an incredible support system. I have people I can love and they love me. Not all of this is guaranteed to anyone. So take a moment to reflect, to pause and really think about what you have that so many probably do not. It can even be the simplest of things, i.e. 'I'm incredibly grateful that I have access to clean water.' I find a great way to do this is to actively seek things to be grateful for during my day. Naturally over the course of a day, good things and bad things can happen, so take a moment after each good thing and say out loud how thankful you are for what just happened. Then take the bad parts, the minor inconveniences, and seek ways to be thankful for them – did they open up an opportunity, perhaps? Did you learn something useful from this? By doing this you are opening your mind to a positive mindset. And, as we've discussed, positivity will breed more positivity into your life.

GET OUT OF YOUR OWN WAY

> 'Experiencing gratitude activates neurotransmitters like dopamine, which we associate with pleasure, and serotonin, which regulates our mood. It also causes the brain to release oxytocin, a hormone which induces feelings like trust and generosity, which promotes social bonding and feeling connected.'
>
> AMY E. KELLER, PSYD

My favourite way to practice gratitude is with a gratitude journal:

I suggest you purchase a little notebook that you can keep by your bed. This will be your gratitude journal, or, alternatively, simply write this on your phone. I want you to think of all the things you were grateful for today just before you go to bed. You can even write down what things you're grateful for for the next day too. I recommend you do this every day, because when you do this regularly, it can give you regular dopamine hits and will also get you in the mindset of looking out for reasons to be happy and grateful throughout your day. You may even feel happier instantly from looking at your life with this more positive outlook.

BUILD SELF-ESTEEM WHEREVER POSSIBLE

We must find happiness here and now or we never will when we complete all our goals and bring all our wildest dreams to life. Yes, you'll feel great, but it won't last, so use gratitude right now and during your journey, because this is the only true way to be happy and ensure happiness in your future. I can't stress this enough; this is such an important step in your timeline. Find happiness now before you've achieved anything, and you won't be coerced into acting and striving for the wrong things and for the wrong reasons. When you strive for achievements that don't need to happen in order for you to find future happiness, you'll be less distracted, less desperate and more likely to actually achieve this success.

The dangerous human lives by their own code

The dangerous human is dangerous because they are different to the majority. Most of us will allow our own feelings or lack thereof to dictate our lives: we make decisions based on insecurity and fear, we comply and try not to rock the boat and, unfortunately, this has so many of us stuck and disappointed in what's around us and what we've accumulated so far with our lives. But the dangerous human lives by their own code, they are self-assured and go for what they want. This is not the norm. They've done this by building rock-solid self-esteem, as they had fears but faced them anyway, and they've grown confidence through action. They are aware of their emotions and know how to express them or how to control some of them through mindfulness. They are happy and know that, in personal growth, they can add more to their lives. The dangerous human is capable of doing anything, but it's entirely in your hands if you want to become a dangerous human too. As with anything in life, no one is coming around the corner to make you incredible, no one is going to give you the title of a dangerous human, so you need to work on all of this to become one, and it's on you. But the rewards, again, are worth it.

9

BE YOU AS MUCH AS YOU CAN

Sometimes life makes you think you need to be someone else. We have endless interactions throughout our lives and, if you're anything like me, you might have a tendency to want people to like you. But not everyone can and not everyone will. Sometimes you like someone romantically but you're not their type, sometimes a boss or colleague just doesn't seem to get you or see how great you are, and sometimes you'll meet new people and they'll be mean or rude to you through no fault of your own. These experiences can happen to any of us. Unfortunately, the default response to these situations is to try to change ourselves, try to be something or someone else to impress them and win them over. The problem with this is we aren't being our true selves, we aren't being honest with who we are, and we are damaging our self-esteem by being okay with changing who we are for others. In this chapter I want to show you ways in which you can be more who you truly are and how not to shy away from this because no one is like you: you are unique, and this is your power.

When I was younger, if I went through a breakup and they said it was because of who I was. I then spent the next three months trying to eradicate the parts of me she had commented on so that it wouldn't happen again. Similarly, when I was growing up, I would watch certain actors on TV and in movies and think they were so cool, which would lead me to think I *wasn't* cool, and so I would do my best to change my personality to match those people (or, rather, characters) on TV. Damn you, Ryan Reynolds!

Both of these examples caused me to have a disjointed personality, with half being genuinely me and half being a bad impression of a Canadian actor. I did this to make people like me because I didn't think that I, just as I was, was good enough. But the problem with this, even when it worked, was that they weren't liking me, at least not the real me. This definitely caused some self-esteem issues down the line. Especially because I was taking an axe to part of my personality to get rid of something that one person didn't like, something that, quite easily, someone else might have liked. What I should have done is been more aware of the fact that it is perfectly normal and okay that one person doesn't like me, and if I was still fixated on people liking me, then I should have sought out the ones that actually liked me and spent less time worrying about a few that didn't.

Ideally, I should have been the most authentic version of myself I could be. Because anything less led me into uncomfortable situations precisely because I wasn't authentic, and then I wound up either hurt, not trusted or lost.

Stop apologising for being you

If you are constantly apologising for being you, this probably means that you genuinely think, deep down in your gut, that you're a failure. A constant need to apologise and say I'm sorry to everyone for everything is more than likely because someone in your life has made you believe that everything bad that has happened is your fault, and so somewhere in your mind and body you truly believe that. Because in your past someone has made you feel like their emotional state is dependent on you and your actions, you now feel that you're ultimately responsible for how someone else feels. But that is not the case, that is trauma at work – childhood trauma, at its finest, in fact – and you have taken it upon your shoulders. Believing that everything that goes wrong in personal relationships is your fault is such a bad place to be mentally and, when you're in it, you don't feel like there are any other solutions because of this trauma and low self-esteem. You will live a tough life if you think you need to apologise for everything and say sorry for being you.

So, to start unpicking this, I want you to stop and remember how amazing you are. I want you to remember that you are doing everything you can do to live, grow and survive, and

I want you to remind yourself that other people's feelings are beyond your control. Feelings are opinions wrapped in emotion. All you can do is work with what you have learned from experience and how you were raised. And, ultimately, all you can do is good enough. Yes, we can learn to grow and be better people, but that doesn't mean apologising for who you are in the moment, who you are now. You don't need to apologise and try to change yourself for someone else, but you do need to work on the trauma that has caused this toxic way of thinking.

I've discussed it before, but therapy is a great way to work through this and can really make a difference. It's a part of the process of getting out of old ways of thinking. The sooner you get more comfortable with exactly who you are, the more life opens up. You'll allow yourself to be judged by others without caring, you'll allow yourself to be honest, and you'll find out why living an honest life is so important. If someone doesn't like you for you, then this is perfectly fine, and they can dislike you from a distance because they don't need to be in your life. Don't give up on yourself. Never think your existence is a burden to anyone; you are loved, and you can learn to love yourself. And never apologise for being yourself, because you are perfect just as you are.

BE YOU AS MUCH AS YOU CAN

Stop hiding your true self (and why, if you do, it has long-term negative effects)

Sometimes, in order to avoid having to say sorry, people will just hide their true selves altogether. They won't be open about who they are and they'll either be a muted version of themselves or try to be someone else entirely. We've already discussed the link between trauma and how this can mean you are not okay being you, but this still doesn't stop some from resorting to hiding who they are, mostly for fear of rejection, and it usually has devastating consequences.

As I've said before, in the past I've definitely not liked who I was. I thought I wasn't cool enough or funny enough, and that nobody would like me unless I was, so I would put on an act and pretend to be someone who wasn't dealing with low self-esteem. I'd do this to make people like me and the unfortunate thing is that they *did* like this version of me (of course they did, it was an act!). I was taking what I thought they would like in a person and then becoming that person, so there was always a good chance that they'd like this version of me, but in doing this I was hiding my true self. This is, plainly and simply, manipulation. I would never think of myself as a manipulative person, because I don't think I'm a bad person, but your reasoning for hiding yourself and changing that for someone else doesn't matter: it is still, in a way, lying to get what you want.

I couldn't hide my true self for ever, though, and eventually these people that I had tricked into liking me got to see the real me. It happened slowly in small bits, or sometimes I had a big 'moment' and they would see it all, but either way, the truth trickled out. Being someone else is incredibly hard, because we are not able to hold the mask up for too long before it slips. And once it's out in the open, one of two things happen: they still like the real version of you but now have some issues around trusting you or they don't like the real you and they don't want anything to do with you, which is what happened to me in a few of my relationships. Either way, I'd screwed up something that could have been good for me if I had just been honest from the start. In the latter case, one of the negatives is that you have been pouring time and energy into a relationship that could otherwise have been saved with someone who was happy to accept the real you, which is another benefit of being honest from the start.

Psychologist Mark Travers, who is the curator of the popular mental health and wellness website, Therapytips, wrote an article in *Forbes* about this: 'We are often afraid to be our authentic selves, even though being seen and accepted for who we are is, arguably, what we desire most. What often drives inauthentic behaviour in relationships is the fear of rejection. This fear can force us to bend over backwards and become someone else entirely.'

We are so counterintuitive; we are desperate to be loved for who we actually are and yet the fear of rejection counters that and we end up faking it. To find a real, deep and intimate connection with anyone, we must be 100% ourselves. And I can tell you from experience, when you find someone who loves you, the real you, you'll realise how inauthentic all your previous experiences were. Be you and be free.

Understanding the importance of your uniqueness and weirdness

Most connections we make, from childhood to all the way into adulthood, are often born out of some kind of niche. We meet people and the best connections tend to come from something that we both enjoy, or both encompass. For example, small similarities, like favourite TV shows or favourite snacks, to larger bonds, such as an active interest in saving the planet or a love for long-distance hiking. From there, we can go on to connect on a number of metrics and attributes, but initially, it's usually this similarity in our more specific tastes, interests or lifestyles that draws us in closer with other people as it's rarer to find people who share our love of these things.

I believe this rareness is not helped by hiding our unique loves. To us it can feel insular to be obsessed with a certain genre of TV and we subconsciously might not share that love with others because we think they won't be interested. But we shouldn't dull down who we are and hide what makes us interesting because we want to meet people like us, people who could potentially be the best of companions or partners, as hiding ourselves means they don't get to really meet us and our nicheness.

Amy Bucher's study on 'authenticity as a path to happiness' has shown that being true to yourself improves brain health and leads to greater life satisfaction. I believe that this is because we almost feel trapped when we can't express our true selves; the fear of being judged and, potentially, the ramifications of hiding our true selves from people close to us. The problem with this is we will always feel uncomfortable in our own skin, there will always be this niggling incompleteness, and this is no way to live.

Society and social media have a funny way of making us think there is something called 'normal', a set standard, and we should all follow it. This usually happens with trends for clothing, TV shows and even food. Advertising for all of these is slipped into our daily lives through our phones, as companies buy advertising space in the form of influencers that we follow, and that, sometimes, is often enough to have us believing that this is what we want, because it seems popular and then that thing becomes the new normal, for a little while anyway.

But this is a load of crock, because *nobody* is normal. Everyone has their own weird side and their likes and dislikes; everyone has weird quirks. Repressing your weird self, hiding who you actually are, doesn't help you – it actually hinders you. In fact, keeping your weirdness to yourself often has a negative effect on your personal freedom and happiness. This is because being inauthentic or lying about who we are for the most part feels uncomfortable. People aren't happy pretending to be someone else, we are happiest when we are ourselves. How much freer would you feel if you were completely honest about your desires and no longer cared what people thought? And then if you could have them love and accept you for these honesties?

It's such an irony in life that we should hide our desires so that we aren't judged by people we don't care about, but the people we do care about may genuinely love us more for our true self if we gave them the chance. I was incredibly nervous when I told people that I was making TikTok videos, regardless of the fact that the videos were aimed to help people, because I cared what those people thought and I was worried it would cause me embarrassment if they weren't supportive. Thankfully, it was all in my head, as no one who cared for me found it at all embarrassing and I was only offered words of encouragement.

If you want to pursue a particular path or live a unique life, away from society's recommendations, then just trust that you are doing the right thing. Provided what you're doing, or whatever your behaviours are, don't hurt anybody else, then only you get to have a say in what makes you happy. Move to Bali and set up the beach bar. Decide that having children is not for you despite the pressure from your family. If it feels right, then that's the path you take. So, instead of focusing on 'will people think I'm weird?', focus on whether you are doing what's best for you now and for your future self.

A great way to start coming out of your shell and getting more comfortable with being your true self is by finding those people with the same unique qualities and interests. Especially if it's a hobby or a goal.

> Look for groups that follow whatever it is that interests you. Start by looking online – Facebook and Instagram are great for finding groups in your area – and then go to them with an open mind, ready to share, and while it may seem scary, you should also go to places where likeminded individuals hang out. Search for meetups that involve your interest. Sharing your passions like this is great way to connect with similar people and this will, in turn, help you connect better with yourself and help you better understand who you truly are in the long term.

Honestly, the world would be such a dull place if everyone was the same, if everyone followed the same interests and we all thought the same. We need diversity, we need outside-of-the-box thinking, we need weirdness. Otherwise, nothing interesting or new would be created. It is up to us to create new and exciting experiences for ourselves and we won't be able to do that with the same thinking we've followed already, so it's time to embrace our weirdness and be completely comfortable with who we are. Use your uniqueness to create something incredible. And we start this by being completely honest with ourselves and others.

BE YOU AS MUCH AS YOU CAN

The importance of being 100% honest with others (and how this opens doors)

Honesty used to be what I feared the most. Growing up, the idea of telling people how I really felt was terrifying. I couldn't tell my dad how his aggression made me feel or how I felt about him, and this then bled over into not being able to be honest in my feelings with my friends. If I didn't like something they did, I would be silent. Then, later, in my teens and early twenties, I could never tell a girl that I liked her, as the idea of being that open, that vulnerable and that honest was terrifying. And all the while I couldn't be honest with myself either. I couldn't tell myself where I needed improvement because I was too busy trying to be something else, something perfect. I would then go on to be anything other than my true self and would act like someone else, someone with different thoughts and feelings. That way, I didn't have to worry about my true feelings and could just ignore them. But all this was before I discovered the power that honesty could have.

Imagine your life as a corridor with multiple doors. The doors are only slightly open – they are mostly ajar and you aren't ever sure if you can go through them or not. They all have question marks on them and you may never get to see on the other side because you're unsure of whether you can go through them. Being dishonest means you will never truly know what is on the other side of the doors. You're stuck in the hallway, unsure what path to take. Honesty brings clarity and clarity brings decisiveness, so being honest gives you the knowledge re whether you can open that door or not. You asked the question, you told people how you felt, and you got an answer to the questions you've always longed for. Sometimes the door will shut, but at least you know and can move on to the next door. You're moving through your life of doors instead of floating in-between with no real knowledge or purpose.

The moment I started to be honest with my thoughts and feelings, doors started to open and close all over the place. One of the major ones was I was honest with myself about my lifestyle at the time. I was partying and drinking too often and, as a result, I felt bad about myself, mentally and physically. I was not in good shape and was constantly anxious, and so I accepted that I needed to make changes, which I did. I cut down on the drinking, started exercising more and started journalling.

I also ended relationships because I was honest with myself and them about what I wanted. I used to keep relationships going for much longer than they should have because I couldn't be honest with how I felt about that person. And, equally, I have created other incredible relationships and friendships because I was honest with them too, about what I wanted.

When I met my partner, I flat out told her that I liked her, something I never used to be so forthcoming with. Being vulnerable in this way is scary, but it is one of the single best things I have ever done. It has created opportunities I never thought possible, like writing this book! Being honest, vulnerable and then being completely okay with the answer have got me further in life than doing anything else. You literally tell yourself what you want, then you go out and do that thing.

BE YOU AS MUCH AS YOU CAN

If it involves telling someone how you feel, then you do that. The door will either open because of your vulnerability or it will close, and if it does close, then you move on to the next opportunity and do the same.

Author Mark Manson said it best in this extract from his book *Models*: 'So, the catch is that everything you say must be as authentic as possible. The more nervous it makes you, the better, because it means you're being authentic and making yourself vulnerable. How attractive you are is based on your confident behaviour. Your confident behaviour is based on how vulnerable you're able to make yourself. And how vulnerable you're able to make yourself is based on how honest you are to yourself and others.'

It all starts with honesty, honesty with yourself first (what do you want?), then, if it involves others, you must be open and honest with them. Do not shy away from being this vulnerable with others because otherwise you'll never truly know what could have been. Ask and you will receive.

> So, take a moment out of your day to do this: I want you to look inward. Look at your life and find where you need to be more honest. This is self-reflection: acknowledge your struggles and then write all of this down in your notebook or journal. Ask yourself these questions: what isn't working? What needs to change? What do you really want? Having this written down means you can then form a plan about how you can change to be more honest with yourself and others.

Honesty and vulnerability are so much more attractive, and I don't just mean that in a dating scenario, as people are naturally drawn to those who can be honest about their own shortcomings, but first you need to acknowledge them yourself.

Being honest is best for you and everyone else involved. There is a power in saying: 'I am me, here it is, this is what I want and I'm going for it.' This simple act opens doors, it opens you to growth, avoids timewasting and it builds some of the most rewarding and fulfilling relationships you will ever have.

Understanding how much effect you have on others (in a positive way)

> 'The effect you have on others is the most valuable currency there is.'
>
> JIM CARREY

When you can be yourself, when you can trust and love yourself, you aren't just helping yourself, you will help others too. Being able to be your truest self will allow you happiness and confidence you never thought possible, and you'll have more motivation to do the things you love. And from that position you will inspire people. I have helped more people in the last four years, since beginning my channels, than I ever had in the previous 31. Despite going into a social media career

BE YOU AS MUCH AS YOU CAN

with the aim of helping people, I wouldn't have been able to do so successfully if I didn't think this was what I was made to do. I found myself at such ease and happiest when I was able to help someone who was struggling and then saw them resolve it with the help of my advice. If I hadn't found myself, understood my own struggles and been open to sharing them, then I wouldn't have been able to be successful in this, and now I have millions of people seeing my content daily, looking for inspiration for their own life.

You will always have an effect on other people, whether that's your vibration or mood. How you feel about yourself will then reflect out into the world, and when you are at the top of your game, by following the points we discuss in this chapter and finding yourself along the way, you will be able to have an enormously positive effect on people. You will do everything you set out to do better and with more purpose. Because there's a good chance you'll be in a happier and healthier place mentally. This could be in something creative like teaching a yoga and meditation class or by starting an inspirational vlog, and then your work will naturally have an effect on people, or it could just be how you feel about yourself being in a more positive light and then your daily interactions with everyone will have a positive knock-on effect.

> So, as all my high school teachers would say, 'I want you to get your thinking caps on' and start having a think about what this could be. Write down ways you want

> to have a positive effect on others, such as starting an inspirational project, and ways you can simply offer more positivity to others, such as complimenting a stranger on what they are wearing. When you have your goals listed, I recommend keeping a tally or writing down when you do these positive acts, as a way to keep you in check and to stay consistent. You can even add what came of your positive act.

The more positivity you give out, the more you tend to receive in return. For example, when interacting with service staff, I'm always complimentary and kind, and this has sometimes meant I've received positivity back or even free items from the staff. I know this is only a minor example, but the power of positivity, and the effect of yours, can be enormous on others.

This can be seen when we spend time with other people who are naturally positive. A close friend of mine is always quick to compliment others and look for positives in what I find myself moaning to them about. I often look to spend as much time with this person as I can, because their company is refreshing and makes me feel lifted. If you can develop a more positive energy and outlook on life, other people will naturally be drawn to you. Another great way to develop this outlook is to actually spend time with people who are already more positive than you.

A Psychology Today article written by academic director of

Columbia University, Dan Tomasulo Ph.D., shows us we can harness the power of positivity by being close to other positive people: 'When you are surrounded by people who radiate positivity, it becomes easier for you to adopt the same mindset. You begin to see the world through a more optimistic lens and start to believe that good things are possible.'

Look out for positive people in your life and learn from them, because when you are comfortable and proud of who you are, you'll find you are increasingly more positive about your life and what you can do. When you do the work on your self-esteem, follow your own ambitions and care less about what people think, then you'll have the self-pride to be a better friend, you'll be a better partner, a better leader, with all of this helping you to live a life of purpose. If you can change and help the way others think and feel because of how good you feel, then you will be rich in life in more ways than one.

Giving yourself the benefit of the doubt in the same way we give this to others

Why are we so harsh on ourselves? 'Alex, you dick, why didn't you get that work done that you said you would?' 'Why did you spend the whole day on the sofa when you said you'd go to the gym?' 'You're not going anywhere with your life!' These are all very real thoughts and things I've said to myself when I didn't do something that I felt I should have done and, to be honest, while I do believe I 'should' have done these things, to speak to myself in this tone or manner is never helpful.

The problem is that when we speak to ourselves in this manner, it attacks our self-esteem and can have a negative effect on our ability to finish tasks. This can't be allowed to happen when we are trying to grow or build something. While we can't just not finish the task, we can definitely take breaks, and it's here that I want you to focus. I want you to be able to give yourself a break and give yourself the benefit of the doubt by genuinely believing in yourself that taking a break doesn't mean you won't finish it, and then, in turn, you do not need to be such an inner critic. Would I ever speak to a friend or loved one in this way? Absolutely not! It's not constructive and it will only cause more mental health issues, because as we already know, negative thoughts about ourselves will have a long-lasting effect on us. When it comes to the people we care about, or even strangers, for that matter, we usually lean towards giving them the benefit of the doubt. And this is something we all need to do for ourselves too. Give yourself that benefit of the doubt that you will get done everything you need to.

If our friend said to themselves that they wanted to go to the gym but didn't manage to go, then we would be reassuring and tell them it's okay, that they'll go tomorrow, i.e. 'it's okay to have off days', 'your mental health needs that break'. But why, when it comes to ourselves, are we so aggressive, harsh and lacking in compassion?

According to McLean Hospital in their article on 'What Is Self-Compassion and How Can We Cultivate It?': 'People may resist self-compassion because they confuse it with selfishness or self-pity. They may feel guilty for being kind to themselves.'

This is counterproductive because then we are never putting ourselves first. We will allow leniencies for others and never for ourselves, which can put us into a spiral of self-criticism. The reasoning might be because we think we will finally do something if we are harsher on ourselves, but then the opposite happens, because the negative berating of oneself then lowers our self-confidence. We have to allow ourselves to make mistakes and to have breaks.

As long as you are looking to push yourself regularly, and you have a great timeline in place, then that's incredible. This is new to you and you're going to have off days. Days when you just can't do as much as you want to, when it just doesn't happen, and I need you to give yourself a break when these times occur. In my creative work, if I try to force a workday when I really can't face it, then the work I produce will be crap. The same goes for a close music artist friend – he always tells me 'You can't force it', and he's the biggest artist in his genre in the world.

Our mental health can only take so much, and you do need breaks. Sometimes those breaks might not have been planned, though, and our mental state forces our hand. We need to apply this same concept to making mistakes. If someone close to you makes a mistake, you don't scold them. Instead, you help them and support them. You need to start doing this for yourself. You will make mistakes every now and then, and maybe even more often now you're pushing yourself into new ventures.

Just do your best not to berate yourself or you will either be forced to break in another way, because your body has broken down, or your stress will become too much, and you'll never be able to create what you set out to do. Go for it all, but be kind to yourself along the journey. You're doing really great by just going for it, so be proud of yourself: you'll get it done.

Not hiding your true self

No one is you. This is an incredible concept: no one can ever be exactly like you, and that means you have value and you have something to show the world. Promise yourself that you won't hide your true self. Promise yourself you won't squish 'you' down, either to impress others or to conform to a norm that you don't necessarily feel comfortable with. Express who you are and do not shy away from it. If you don't show the world who you are, then you are missing out: embrace your nicheness and find others who share these interests, as this will help you build yourself up and help you to become comfortable with your true self. Find ways to be positive and then share that positivity with others, as positivity breeds more positivity, and interesting experiences can be found through this. This world needs you; we need you to be honest about what you want, honest with the people you love, and when you are living a completely authentic life, you will be a far happier person. Through complete honesty you will save yourself wasting your

BE YOU AS MUCH AS YOU CAN

time and that of others, and you will find what is actually right for you. Be that positive person who can have an incredible impact on this world. Be good to yourself, be kind to yourself, try not to berate yourself when you need a break, and trust you will get what needs to be done, done. Be you, *all* of you.

10

DO EVERYTHING ALONE

Do you remember when you were in school and the teacher would say something like 'Okay, for this next project I want you to get into groups.' As a kid, whenever I heard this, I'd be so much happier, not just because I might be able to work with my friends but also because facing a challenge as a group was so much easier. It meant I didn't have to do all the work and, to be honest, it meant the result of the project didn't mean that much to me either. If we did well then we looked like an intelligent group, but if we didn't do well then at least I wasn't holding the blame for being useless, because we had all messed up, right?

The same happens in places of work, as working on a project as a team means everyone is bringing different perspectives and different skill sets together to tackle a challenge. But what is often forgotten about, and is a stumbling block for group projects, is a lack of accountability. Not one person can be blamed, so that takes the pressure off each member. We naturally like this comfort blanket, as it makes us feel safe. But when it comes to building something with our lives, or even just improving it, we are often faced with doing it alone, and a group can't help us do it. It's all up to us: we are solely accountable, and we tend to shy away from that. This is all for you, though. We're doing this for our own lives, so we have to be accountable and, for the most part, we must do this alone.

This is the lonely chapter, I'm afraid. Come in . . . make yourself at home. I've sat in this room too. But, while it may seem empty, I want to assure you that there are millions of people in here too. You can't see them, but they're here, right there with you, maybe right now. Anyone who has ever wanted to do something with their life has been here or is currently here. This is the lonely abyss, where the people around you don't quite understand what you're trying to do. Maybe you don't fit in with the way of thinking shared by those that you normally surround yourself with? Whatever it is, you haven't quite found the success you're looking for yet. You don't fit into a new place or with new people, or maybe the process is taking so much of your time that you don't have the time for the old you, the old habits and even the people that you'd usually distract yourself with.

To do a little recap of what we've learned so far . . . you will work your butt off, plan your timeline, stick to it religiously, you'll use your past trauma as motivation and finally get past it, understand your ego and refocus it, face and overcome all the failure this journey encompasses, you'll 'pull out the weeds',

DO EVERYTHING ALONE

end the distractions and become a 'dangerous human'. And now you understand how you're going to do all of these, you have to get comfortable with the concept of radical accountability. You're going to do all of this and it's going to be incredible, but you've got to do it alone. You have to take this adventure on your own because it is only you who can make it succeed. The hidden secret to success in any area of life is that, in order to achieve it, it will consume so much of you and ask that you do what you feel is best over what others choose, and this will naturally make you feel lonely. But once you accept this, you'll be able to do whatever you want.

Understanding that you are on your own and you always have been

You've always been on your own. You may not realise it because, when you're a child, if you're lucky (because not everyone has this luxury), your parents will have cared for you, guided you and paid your way. But from the moment you left the bubble of home for other worlds (whether that be preschool, kindergarten, nursery or any other place outside of your parents' immediate care), you have been on your own. Yes, there's guardians and teachers to make sure you don't do anything stupid or hurt yourself, and they help guide you in what you should or need to be doing, but it's been you that has been doing what you need to for yourself. *You* had to go make friends, *you* had to communicate your wants and needs, *you* had to work out which shape went into the square hole (literally and metaphorically). This continues throughout your life: when you're in high school or secondary school, you have to make your own decisions, you decide how you apply yourself, you decide how you'll be socially. Of course, experience and trauma (like, for instance, not being shown the correct love as a child and then subsequently growing up with no self-confidence) will have its say, but at the end of the day it is you experiencing all of this and you alone. It may have felt nice to have the shelter of your parents or guardians at home, but it was more of an oversight than a practical protection. They didn't go to school for you, they didn't do the work, they didn't make your day-to-day decisions for you, which ultimately had a long-lasting effect on you.

We are creatures of habit and like to repeat what we know, so it's highly likely that how we experienced our school years will bleed into adulthood. If we have spent that time looking for others to protect us or if we spent those years not being accountable for our behaviour or actions, then it's highly likely we will continue to do this going into adulthood. What ideally would have happened as kids growing up would be that we were faced with challenges that we solved ourselves. This would have built our self-esteem and made us resilient to the hardships that life throws at us, including supporting ourselves as adults. But this may not have happened, and we don't have a time machine and can't magically give ourselves these formative challenges in our childhoods, which means that, to

DO EVERYTHING ALONE

make us resilient now and help us get used to being alone and accountable for ourselves, we need new experiences and new challenges to help us build this sense of accountability. And this is exactly what we are doing here.

So, you might feel lonely right now, taking on this new adventure, this new world, these new experiences that, quite frankly, scare the crap out of you, but in the act of doing this we are helping ourselves to understand the concept of doing everything alone. And while this may all seem like fresh ground, fear not, because you will have definitely done some things in the past on your own. Unless you're the only person on Earth who has never made a single decision for themselves and has been led entirely by other people, then there's a good chance you've made difficult decisions already on your own. Two people can't make a decision for one person unless that person is happy to relinquish control, and even if that does happen to you, it can't be the case with absolutely everything in your life. Nobody has made as many decisions as you have about your life. Once you understand this, you may just start to believe that you have actually got to this point on your own, so you really can do this now.

No one is coming to save you or make it all better

How long have you sat there waiting? Waiting for it all to be okay, waiting for it all to work out? I'm not going to lie – I sat there for a while. I was going through the motions of life: friends, parties, relationships, work, never taking anything further, not building anything great but always secretly hoping that something would just change, and that I'd suddenly be wealthy and mentally a lot happier. I was never actively doing anything to create that, though; I just waited for the change, thinking somehow it would happen. But if I wasn't making moves that would bring these positives into my life, then who did I expect to bring them to me?

There's a multi-million-pound company that prays on this way of thinking. Some people aspire to great sums of wealth but don't want to do the work themselves to receive it, and this company takes advantage of those people. Its patrons just hope and pray that wealth and success will happen to them, and this company takes millions in return. In the UK, it's called the National Lottery, but there are similar schemes in other countries. These schemes sell the dream of financial riches to the people who want it most, usually the poorest of people, usually the most vulnerable, people who really don't think they can ever achieve anything like this level of financial wealth, so leave it up to the fate of a lottery.

The sense of helplessness in this model is tough, but the problem is not just isolated to the lottery. Many of us wish for promotions in our workplaces but we don't push ourselves to do the work required for that promotion. Many of us (including the old me) believe we are deserving of love and a successful relationship without understanding or applying the work that creates that. We all know that you're statistically more than

DO EVERYTHING ALONE

likely to be struck by lightning twice than you are to win the lottery, so as someone in the room that's never been struck, I'll go out on a limb and say that I don't think I'm going to win the lottery. But I also don't think anyone is going to give us the promotion we might long for unless we apply ourselves and, from my own experience, I also believe it's unlikely anyone will want to be in a loving, long-term relationship with us unless we understand what it takes to have this. This is on us: we must understand precisely what we want, and we have to take action on that. This is how you win your lottery in life.

And just as you shouldn't defer to the universe to give you what you want, also you cannot rely on other people to tell you. You cannot get advice on what you should do with your life, what field you should go into or what person you should date. Nobody knows but you, nobody has a grasp on who you are, what makes you tick, what your interests are, what motivates you and how you think. Heck, sometimes *you* don't even know who you are, so how are you going to sit there and wait for someone else to make it all better if they don't know you or if they don't understand you?

Thinking someone else will make your dreams come true is fantasy. You need to make the decisions, and you need to make the moves. Not everyone will agree or understand, but that doesn't matter, because it's you that's making these decisions, just as it always has been. You are doing this alone, as it's your life and nobody will come along and change that once you realise it's all on you.

As we discussed in Chapter 1 – Acknowledge and Design

Your Own Timeline, it's okay to trust the process, but only if you've put that process in motion and you're taking steps towards your goals.

The bottom line is: no one is coming. No one is coming to tell you to turn the TV off or to stop scrolling on your phone, no one is coming to tell you to exercise, no one is coming to help you build your business plan. Also, while I can tell you throughout this book that you should change, it's still you who decides that you want change; it's you who reads the words and then actually takes the action. We need to become the parent we discussed at the beginning, the one that we always imagined as our comfort blanket because they helped and guided us. No one is here to guide us, so we are now our own guides, telling ourselves what we need to do to change our life for the better. I know it's in you. I know you can do this because I was someone who didn't want to do the hard stuff but who learned to parent myself into being successful. It is possible – you can do it, but just get comfortable with the fact that no one else is coming to help, and you have to do it yourself.

How you are of no help to anyone unless you believe in yourself

You're doing this for you, and to create an incredible life for yourself, and, for the most part, we are doing this alone, but it's worth bearing in mind that, at some point, other people

DO EVERYTHING ALONE

will need to be involved. You might need something from others, such as some insight from someone who has gone through this task before. Maybe the next exciting thing in your life is pushing yourself to meet new people, socially or romantically? Maybe you want to build a business or go for what you want in your career, and so you'll need to inspire people you work with or take on employees with skills you don't have for your business?

Regardless of what it is you wish to achieve, there will inevitably have to be some form of human interaction along the way. You will have to show yourself to others at some point and it will be important for your success to have confidence in yourself while doing so. If not, then those people won't be inspired, they won't be impressed, and they will be wary of your authenticity in the interaction. This could then mean they won't buy into what you're selling, as it were, and if the result of what you're doing depends on people buying into you, well, without self-belief you will not succeed.

If you go through this journey being shy or being unsure about yourself or what you're doing, your lack of self-confidence will show through and people will be less likely to offer you that job, hesitant to help finance your business ideas, give you the role you want or generally believe in you. You have to believe in yourself before others can believe in you, and you are of no help to anyone in this world until you do.

Imagine, for example, you're on a first date and the person sitting across from you can't hold eye contact. They seem visibly nervous to talk to you and they have a tendency to put themselves down. Without a sudden upturn in confidence, there probably won't be a second date because confidence is attractive, but so is connection, and without eye contact or an ability to talk openly and passionately, connection will likely be a struggle. But, also, a lack of confidence suggests deeper insecurities that could cause issues further down the line, and, while everyone has insecurities, the depth and visibility of these issues on the first date doesn't offer a hopeful look at the future.

Sports psychologist Dr TC North, who has consulted with multiple Olympic athletes, believes having greater self-confidence allows you to influence others and had this to say in an article on the benefits of increasing your self-confidence: 'In conversations, in a family situation or in a business situation, when you're on stage as a presenter, when you are confident, people are willing to listen to you, they believe what you say. They give you more credibility, you are perceived with more "cred" with confidence.' This is incredibly useful when you're looking to better your life, as having people around you who believe in what you're doing will help you achieve your goals faster.

Renowned psychologist Albert Bandura found that people who have high self-belief see difficult scenarios as challenges to be overcome rather than something to avoid. He also found that confident people can recover more quickly from setbacks and then respond with determined effort. He says that these responses are incredibly important for long-term success and that, without this self-belief, we open ourselves up to determining failure as a lesson to never try again. People can hear

DO EVERYTHING ALONE

and feel your confidence and your self-belief. When we meet someone with a strong self-belief, it relaxes us and makes us feel comfortable and inspired. This is how you want people to feel around you. You are installing confidence in others.

So, if you have incredible self-belief, then that's fantastic, but don't worry if you don't, because I'll now go into how we can achieve this. To gain self-belief we have to get rid of the opposite: self-doubt. Let's say you want to be healthier, and you want to get into shape, but you just don't think you can cut out sugar. Maybe just thinking about it makes you want some chocolate or maybe you've tried before but the cravings were just too much. Worrying about not being able to cut out sugar in order to be healthier is just a small example of self-doubt, but a lack of belief in yourself will continue to frustrate you and see you not even entertain the challenge, no matter how great the idea is or what you can gain from the opportunity.

So, in order to counteract this, a mindset shift is needed. I challenge you to change your thinking:

> First, I want you to write out all of these insecure thoughts of self-doubt: jot down all the ways and reasons this won't work out. Often what happens when we see these excuses out of our head and written down is that we can actually see the fraudulent nature of them. When read out loud, they start to seem ridiculous because most of the time they lack any proof. Then I want you to write out why you are doing all this. If that is clear, then you

> know exactly what you need to do, and when the why is overly powerful, you will be of a mindset that it has to happen, and you won't accept a life (your life) without the goal being achieved.

When you clear your mind of the self-doubt and then believe that you can, because you want it, then you have self-belief. And this belief is not certain it works perfectly the first time, it doesn't believe we'll ace it, but it's a belief that we are willing to test, fail and try new things, even when we feel uncertain, and this is something I believe that anyone can do, regardless of experience. Anyone can go for it.

The main distinction I've seen between successful and unsuccessful individuals isn't intelligence, opportunity or resources, it's the genuine belief that, whatever happens, they can succeed. However uncertain I am about a task or challenge, I know I just have to go into it regardless and trust that I will figure it out along the way and make it work. I sold houses when I was 18, I became a data engineer at 20, I helped write last will and testaments for a law firm at 22. Before applying for any of those jobs I had absolutely no experience in any of those fields – I just believed in myself that I could make it work; I trusted I would learn and that it would eventually work out. When I find an exciting opportunity that I may not be fully qualified for (which happens often), I still go for it, trusting that I'll figure it out along the way. My belief in myself has made a significant difference repeatedly. I didn't need exceptional intelligence, abundant opportunities, or vast resources – just a simple, unwavering confidence that I can figure it out.

Whatever your aim or your goals are, while being life-changing for yourself, they will also naturally have some kind of knock-on effect on others – maybe your family, friends or partners. They will benefit from your high self-belief, they will trust in you as you trust in yourself, and this will give you greater freedom to perform and succeed without the doubts of others (if you have self-doubt) distracting you or turning your head. You will gain more supporters and fans along the way, which could have great benefit to you in your journey. Trust that you will be able to figure it out, make it work and people will believe in you in return.

How nothing external should affect how you feel or your plans

You need to care less. This is hard to do, because naturally we care about the result of something we are putting effort into, and naturally we care what people will think of that result. But I am here to tell you that, to accomplish something, you're going to have to build a thick skin and care less about outside noise, because if we don't, it will have a negative effect on the outcome or our lives. Our societies are hell-bent on trying to make us give a damn about everything: the news shows us what is happening outside of our immediate spheres and

GET OUT OF YOUR OWN WAY

social media and magazines tell us what the new trends are and why we should care about them. It's difficult not to be influenced in some way unless we completely cut ourselves off from the external world. And caring about every mistake or every person's opinion will slow your process down to a crawl. It may even throw you off course completely and stop what you started. It will have you second-guessing all your steps based on what we presume others will think or what it will look like. The expectation should be that you're proud of yourself and you will succeed regardless, rather than that the end result should be absolutely perfect. And it definitely should not be influenced by whether every single person will like it or approve of it. We need to care less. And to do this we need to change our priorities.

One priority you have right now is that you want to achieve something or be a certain way, whatever that is. It is the reason you picked up this book, but right now there are a few too many other priorities in the way that we need to shuffle to the bottom of the deck or discard altogether.

> Get your notebook out and write down everything you care about. I want you to be completely honest, and it's okay to have things like 'other people's approval' on the list. I just want you to write out all of the things you care about. Once it's all written down, you can change the order of things. At the top you want 'the change', i.e. the thing you're working towards, and at the bottom

DO EVERYTHING ALONE

> of the list you will place things like 'fear of failure' or 'other people's approval'. This is now your list of priorities and you should only focus on the top half. Every day, whenever you have to make important decisions or take steps in a certain direction, you can consult your list of priorities. If the decision or move is in line with the top half of the priorities, then make it. If it is more in line with the bottom half of the list – for example, doing something to gain the approval of others – then it probably shouldn't be done. To care less is to care more for what is actually important to us.

I had a friend who was killed recently – while I was writing this book, actually. Out of respect for them and their family, I won't go into details, but I bring it up because death is a great reminder of what is important in life and what you should prioritise. I often find myself giving a crap about how I'll be perceived if I do this or say that, but then I think about those people I know that have passed on and how they'd probably slap me for not *living*, if they could. Because we are not living a life if we make every move while caring too much about insignificant stuff, such as what strangers think of us or if everyone will understand us. If we get to have a deathbed experience one day instead of being taken unexpectedly, it's highly unlikely we'll think 'I'm glad I cared what all those people thought and didn't potentially make a fool of myself by going for that career I wanted, I'm glad I played it safe.' No, this almost definitely *won't* be the case.

GET OUT OF YOUR OWN WAY

Whatever it is that you seem to find yourself prioritising over actually going out there and achieving something can't stand up to the present moment. Right now you are here, you're alive, and you have made it through all your past anxieties, such as those about other people's opinions. It might not be so obvious in the present moment, but it almost always works out. You will fail and you will win, people will care and people won't, but it will work out in the end. You can use your current knowledge that everything has worked out so far as a tool to care less about outside noise and anxieties around other people's thoughts. Even in cases where you might have been sad because of something you've experienced, that too was in your control. If you've come away from it alive, then everything still keeps moving – the world keeps rotating and everyone else gets on with their life, so you can as well.

Your journey and what you're looking to achieve or change is now your main priority, so care less about outside noise and care more for what the journey and the result will do for your life. You'll have a great story to tell, all the while rounding yourself out as a better, more experienced human. If you let anxiety win, if you let it take control, you'll never get out of your own way. There will always be some kind of self-doubt or some made-up scenario where it goes horribly wrong in your mind. But it usually never does. So care less and live more.

DO EVERYTHING ALONE

This is on you

The biggest mistake I ever made was waiting for the world to make me feel good. When I realised life was not happening to me but rather through me, it all started to make sense. I was in control, and if I could create an unhappy, anxious mindset, then I could also create a happy, curious and successful one. There are two different lives ahead of you, and it's up to you to decide which path you are going to take. The current one, the one that prompted you consciously or unconsciously to pick up this book, or the alternative, the one where you make a plan, push through fear, experience incredible highs, see progress, achieve what you set out to achieve and live a life of purpose. But it is you who has to make this decision, as nobody else is coming to make it for you.

I hope that, with a little help from this book, you can learn how to be you, be comfortable with yourself and never hide the true you. It's my hope that eventually you build self-love, self-belief and, in turn, inner confidence. I hope I have inspired you to reach for your dreams and go for what you want in life. I genuinely believe that, if you follow all the guidance from this book and get out of your own way, you'll be able to create and accomplish incredible things.

People will think what they want to think, and they will more than likely think of how your plans will affect them, but take what you've learned about others and use that to help guide you away from the outside noise, as it's best if we don't let other people's opinions about our life change what we want to do with that life. Setting healthy boundaries and removing the bad apples will hopefully open up new and incredible opportunities. Practising good healthy habits will hopefully build confidence and diminish stress and anxiety too. Use this book to help you find inspiration in the world and within yourself.

Face your fears and, if failure happens, remember to learn from each experience, making your understanding of you and your journey greater. I'm confident you can learn to dismantle your ego and allow yourself to move freely without fear of being judged by others or yourself. Above all, though, I hope I've motivated you to become accountable for everything you do, because I believe this will help you to create a beautiful life for yourself. I have given you the tools, but only you, on your own, can now action everything we have discussed within these pages. I hope it will help you accomplish everything you desire.

And, either way, I know you're going to have an incredible ride with your timelines, because I sure have. I never thought, growing up and in my twenties, that I would become a published author, but this became one of my main goals when I turned 30, so I started creating content with the dream of one day being a published author. And even though I never knew exactly how to go about doing it, I made decisions that I thought would get me going in that direction. I kept my head down and worked hard, I trusted in my timeline and learned from all the ups and downs, all of my successes and all of my failures, and I learned as much as I could. I ignored the internal self-doubt of 'you can't do this, you don't know how to write a book', and

DO EVERYTHING ALONE

I just went into this creative stretch of my life believing that eventually I would be published and I would figure it out as I went along. I used the success from my social media channels to work out what people wanted, worked out how I could help them best, and I wrote that down. All I have left to say is thank you for reading this: you are now part of my timeline and you have just read my dream come to fruition. Now go make your own dream happen. There is *nothing* in your way.

ACKNOWLEDGEMENTS

Much like the butterfly that flaps its wings in Japan and subsequently causes a tornado in Brazil, there are a lot of people – people who have done incredible things in their lives – without whom this book would not exist. So, these people need to be thanked and acknowledged. I'd like to start with my brilliant editor at Headline, Oliver Holden-Rea: you saw something in me and my content, and believed we could write an incredible book. You were not wrong. Thank you for guiding this first-time author through absolutely everything, from answering all my silly questions to helping shape this book, all the while showing constant belief in me and my writing. I can't thank you enough. You are gifted and a master of your craft. What started out as an Instagram DM is now a published book, one that will help people, and so much of that is because of you.

Rebecca, my beautiful partner – I could fill another book

with just how incredible you and the effect you've had on me have been, but to spare the pages and everyone else's time, I will stick to just this: thank you for being so patient with me. While I stressed out and stole time away from us to write this, you were there throughout, filling me with confidence through your love and being the best cheerleader I could ever have asked for. To try and impress you on our first date, I told you I wanted to write a book to help people. Then, when I realised this would turn into a serious relationship, I had to put my money where my mouth was and actually *write* the thing! Thank you for sticking around, my love.

For Grace, my incredible daughter, who, once she was told I was writing a book, decided to ask me how far along I was almost every day . . . Thank you for keeping me accountable, and for being the reason I got my act together. You have changed my life in the best of ways.

For my protective mother, Angela: life has been difficult for you, but you showed strength in return. You did everything you could to show me and my siblings that trauma does not stop us, and that we must keep going. Thank you for teaching me strength and for always making sure we were okay.

For my older brother, Rufus: I have always looked up to you. You took me under your wing in my teens, and while I didn't realise it at the time, you were being a father figure for me. Thank you for guiding me and showing me the world.

For my younger brother, James: you have always worn your heart on your sleeve and are one of the kindest people I know. Anyone who has ever met the both of us has always preferred

ACKNOWLEDGEMENTS

you. I'm not jealous, just proud – thank you for being you, and for letting me rant self-improvement advice at you.

For my best friends, Mark, Joe, Tom and Edd: you have ridden this journey with me since we were little sprogs, so thank you for being such an incredible group of friends, and for allowing the space to talk about our mental health with no judgement or ridicule. You have saved me more than once.

Thank you, also, to everyone at Headline and Welbeck Publishing Group – all those people behind the scenes who have done incredible things to make this the book what it is today.

And, finally, I want to thank my grandmother, Elizabeth: sadly, you're not here to read this, but you were the most beautiful soul to walk this earth. You taught me generosity, compassion and patience. You made me want to do good with this life, so thank you.